Piping Down the Valleys Wild

Piping

POETRY FOR THE YOUNG OF ALL AGES

Down the Valleys Wild

Edited, with a new introduction by NANCY LARRICK

Illustrated by Ellen Raskin

DELACORTE PRESS / NEW YORK

Published by
Delacorte Press
1 Dag Hammarskjold Plaza
New York, N.Y. 10017

Library of Congress Cataloging in Publication Data

The Library of Congress has cataloged the first
printing of this title as follows:

Larrick, Nancy, comp.
Piping down the valleys wild; poetry for the young of all ages,
edited with an introd. by Nancy Larrick. Illustrated by Ellen
Raskin.   New York, Delacorte Press [c1968]

xxiii, 247 p.   illus.   24 cm.   4.95

Summary: An anthology of poems grouped in sixteen parts, each devoted
to a particular subject such as animals, seasons, holidays, and people.

1. Children's poetry.   [1. American poetry—Collections.   2. English poetry
—Collections]   I. Raskin, Ellen, illus.   II. Title.   III. Title: Poetry for the
young of all ages.

PN6110.C4L346   821'.008   67-19762
ISBN 0-385-29429-8   MARC

Library of Congress   AC

To the parents and teachers
who have been my students
and to the hundreds of children
with whom we have read poetry

Contents

1. "I'm shouting

I'm singing

I'm swinging through trees ..."

2. "Sing a song of laughter..."

3. "I like it when it's mizzly..." and just a little drizzly..."

4. "I saw a star slide down the sky..."

5. *"I saw*
   a spooky witch
   out riding on her broom."

6. "I wonder what the spring will shout . . ."

7. "I chanced to meet . . ."

8. "I'd take the hound with the drooping ears..."

9. "I heard a bird sing..."

10. "I found new-born foxes..."

13. "I must go down to the seas again ..."

14. "The city spreads its wings ..."

15. "I was one of the children told . . ."

16. "A dozen dreams to dance to you . . ."

THE PIPER

Piping down the valleys wild,
   Piping songs of pleasant glee,
On a cloud I saw a child,
   And he laughing said to me:

"Pipe a song about a Lamb!"
   So I piped with merry cheer.
"Piper, pipe that song again;"
   So I piped; he wept to hear.

"Drop thy pipe, thy happy pipe;
   Sing thy songs of happy cheer!"
So I sang the same again,
   While he wept with joy to hear.

"Piper, sit thee down and write
   In a book, that all may read."
So he vanished from my sight;
   And I plucked a hollow reed,

And I made a rural pen,
   And I stained the water clear
And I write my happy songs
   Every child may joy to hear.

WILLIAM BLAKE

Piping Down the Valleys Wild

CHILDREN RESPOND EAGERLY TO the sound of language and of music. On radio and television they may hear more oral language than they will be able to read in a lifetime. With almost every television program and commercial they hear the sound of music, and they love it.

This may be one reason why they respond so warmly to poetry. After all, poetry itself is music. As we listen to a poem we may hear the tapping of the rain on the roof or the clackety-clack of a distant train. One poem hums as softly as a lullaby, but another may grab you with the clash-bang of a jazz band.

In William Blake's famous poem "The Piper," he is himself the piper—the one who plays a tune on his flute or perhaps his bag-pipes. The child in Blake's poem is so caught up with the music that he asks to hear it again. And then again. Then he asks for the words to listen to and later to read.

This seems to be the sequence that our children prefer today: listening to the total sound or music of a poem, then hearing the words, and later coming to words "in a book that all may read." Thus the magic of sound draws children into the pleasures of poetry.

Like William Blake, the child who enjoys poetry is ready to go "piping down the valleys wild." This kind of growing up through poetry happens only when it is synonymous with pleasure for the child. The poems children meet should be those that set their hearts dancing.

Piping Down the Valleys Wild is a collection of poems that present-day children enjoy. All have been read to or read by nursery-school and elementary-school children, who have preferred these poems over hundreds of others. Not every poem is endorsed by every child, of course. Some are clearly for the younger children just stepping beyond Mother Goose. Others are for the eleven- and twelve-year-olds, who have a great sense of their emerging maturity. In between are scores of poems that appeal to a wide age-range.

All of the youngsters who helped in the selection of poems for this volume had had some previous acquaintance with poetry—listening to it, chanting repeated lines, reading on their own, and above all commenting on the marks of quality in a poem. In the beginning many of them looked for rhyme as the first requirement of a poem. If it didn't rhyme, they argued, it wasn't a poem.

Gradually they began to listen to the music and to look for fresh ideas and new word-pictures. They noted evidence of the poet's imagination and emotion and their own response as poetry readers or listeners. The early demand for rhyme faded as children learned to enjoy poetry that ranged from unrhymed free verse to ballads, limericks, and rhyming quatrains.

After exploring poetry with hundreds and hundreds of children in recent years, I find them particularly responsive to the simple, almost conversational language of modern verse. They seem to prefer poems that are fresh and crisp over those they consider "too sweet." Again and again a child would say, "I like this one because it's real." Or "I like it because it makes me feel good." What better reason can be given?

Most of the children who voiced their preferences for the poems in this volume live in urban or suburban communities. They know traffic lights and concrete mixers, but they have never met gentians or salamanders. Even country children who travel to school by bus are so influenced by the mass media that they count Michael Jackson among their friends but not the jack-in-the-pulpit. Except in rare cases, poems about bringing in the cows or sliding down a haystack evoke only slight response with either city children or their country cousins.

Most children look for the familiar in a poem and branch out from there. When they meet an image that is out of keeping with their immediate experience, they hesitate. The nostalgic picture of the "small fat grandmamma with a very slippery knee" leaves them unmoved. Their own grandmothers are working or playing golf.

In the realm of fantasy, children are ready to suspend their disbelief more readily. They shiver with pleasure when a poem is about ghosts or ghouls or goblins. Talking animals win almost every child, particularly if they are funny. The humor of "The Owl and the Pussy-Cat" seems to be as popular today as it was when it was created more than a hundred years ago.

Yet for every generalization about children's taste in poetry, there are exceptions. And the more children read or hear poetry, the wider the range of their interpretations and reactions. Each child comes to the poet's image with his own color filter and thus creates something that is his alone. This, after all, is what we hope will happen between poet and child. For a poet will only hint at images and ideas. The listener or reader must re-create them as his own.

Long ago it was said that "what can be explained is not poetry." That is, we can ponder over a poet's lines and bring all of our experience to play on that instrument. But each of us will hear a different message—one that may vary through the years as we gather more experience with things that cannot be explained precisely.

Perhaps this is why poetry has been called the most personal form of literature. Also it may explain why poetry usually needs a special introduction, particularly for children. But it must be a very informal, very personal introduction. The youngest must hear the poem, of course, but even the older ones who read independently respond first of all to the sound of poetry.

After all, poetry is meant to be heard. But as one teacher put it, "Listening isn't what it used to be!" The children of television seem to be able to switch channels as we read to them. They may appear to be listening and not hear a word.

However, when they are drawn into chanting repeated lines or chorus, they are with you. They like to chant the refrain "In the week when Christmas comes" in Eleanor Farjeon's poem. Or to cry out the "Slam, slam, slam" or "Bam, bam, bam" of Eve Merriam's wrecking ball.

With two or three children it is fun to give a spontaneous dramatization of such a poem as "The Old Wife and the Ghost." There are only three characters, of course—the old wife, the ghost, and the "tidy big cat"—but how many sound effects can be produced when that ghost rattles and jangles and bumps and thumps!

Participation seems to make poetry twice as much fun. And invariably it leads to reading.

What really counts is that children develop a love of poetry. This will come about, in most cases, when they have a chance to play with poetry—"to do it," as one child put it—and to meet many kinds of poetry with family or friends who are ready to explore and experiment. I hope you are!

NANCY LARRICK
WINCHESTER, VIRGINIA
NOVEMBER 12, 1984

Piping Down the Valleys Wild

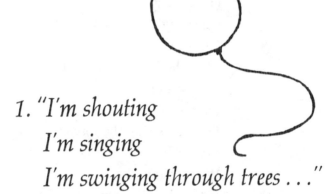

1. "I'm shouting
    I'm singing
    I'm swinging through trees ..."

SPRING

I'm shouting
I'm singing
I'm swinging through trees
I'm winging skyhigh
With the buzzing black bees.
I'm the sun
I'm the moon
I'm the dew on the rose.
I'm a rabbit
Whose habit
Is twitching his nose.
I'm lively
I'm lovely
I'm kicking my heels.
I'm crying "Come dance"
To the fresh water eels.
I'm racing through meadows
Without any coat
I'm a gamboling lamb
I'm a light leaping goat
I'm a bud
I'm a bloom
I'm a dove on the wing.
I'm running on rooftops
And welcoming spring!

KARLA KUSKIN

TIPTOE

Yesterday I skipped all day,
The day before I ran,
Today I'm going to tiptoe
Everywhere I can.
I'll tiptoe down the stairway.
I'll tiptoe through the door.
I'll tiptoe to the living room
And give an awful roar
And my father, who is reading,
Will jump up from his chair
And mumble something silly like
"I didn't see you there."
I'll tiptoe to my mother
And give a little cough
And when she spins to see me
Why, I'll softly tiptoe off.
I'll tiptoe through the meadows,
Over hills and yellow sands
And when my toes get tired
Then I'll tiptoe on my hands.

KARLA KUSKIN

Every time I climb a tree
Every time I climb a tree
Every time I climb a tree
I scrape a leg
Or skin a knee
And every time I climb a tree
I find some ants
Or dodge a bee
And get the ants
All over me

And every time I climb a tree
Where have you been?
They say to me
But don't they know that I am free
Every time I climb a tree?
I like it best
To spot a nest
That has an egg
Or maybe three

And then I skin
The other leg
But every time I climb a tree
I see a lot of things to see

Swallows rooftops and TV
And all the fields and farms there be
Every time I climb a tree
Though climbing may be good for ants
It isn't awfully good for pants
But still it's pretty good for me
Every time I climb a tree.

DAVID MCCORD

THE SWING

How do you like to go up in a swing,
    Up in the air so blue?
Oh, I do think it the pleasantest thing
    Ever a child can do!

Up in the air and over the wall,
    Till I can see so wide,
Rivers and trees and cattle and all
    Over the countryside—

Till I look down on the garden green,
    Down on the roof so brown—
Up in the air I go flying again,
    Up in the air and down!

ROBERT LOUIS STEVENSON

[5]

THE BALLOON

I went to the park
And I bought a balloon.
It sailed through the sky
Like a large orange moon.
It bumped and it fluttered
And swam with the clouds.
Small birds flew around it
In high chirping crowds.
It bounced and it balanced
And bowed with the breeze.
It skimmed past the leaves
On the tops of the trees.
And then as the day
Started turning to night
I gave a short jump
And I held the string tight
And home we all sailed
Through the darkening sky,
The orange balloon, the small birds
And I.

KARLA KUSKIN

KITE

I flew my kite
One bright blue day,
Light yellow-orangey away
Above the tip tall tops of trees,
With little drops from breeze to breeze,
With little rises and surprises,
And the string would sing to these.

I flew my kite
One white new day,
Bright orange-yellowy and gay
Against the clouds. I flew it through
The cloudiness of one or two—
Careering, veering, disappearing;
String to fingers, tight and true.

I flew my kite
One dole-dark day,
Dull orange image in the grey,
When not a single bird would fly
So windy wet and wild a sky
Of little languors and great angers.
Kite, *good-by, good-by, good-by!*

DAVID MCCORD

THE FISHERMAN

The little boy is fishing
With a green fishline,
And he has got me wishing
That his line were mine.

The little boy is fishing
With a fresh-cut pole,
And he has got me wishing
For his fishing hole.

The little boy is fishing
With better than a pin,
And he has got me wishing
That he won't fall in.

The little boy is fishing
With a disenchanted slug,
And he has got me wishing
For the first faint tug.

The little boy is fishing
With a cider-cork float,
And he has got me wishing
For the cider and a boat.

The little boy is fishing
For I don't know what,
And he has got my wishing
In an awful knot.

DAVID MC CORD

THE LITTLE WHISTLER

My mother whistled softly,
My father whistled bravely,
My brother whistled merrily,
And I tried all day long!
I blew my breath inwards,
I blew my breath outwards,
But all you heard was breath blowing
And not a bit of song!

But today I heard a bluebird,
A happy, young, and new bird,
Whistling in the apple tree—
He'd just discovered how!
Then quick I blew my breath in,
And gay I blew my breath out,
And suddenly I blew three wild notes—
And I can whistle now!

FRANCES FROST

I met a man as I went walking;
We got talking,
Man and I.
"Where are you going to, Man?" I said
(I said to the Man as he went by).
"Down to the village, to get some bread.
Will you come with me?" "No, not I."

I met a Horse as I went walking;
We got talking,
Horse and I.
"Where are you going to, Horse, today?"
(I said to the Horse as he went by).
"Down to the village to get some hay.
Will you come with me?" "No, not I."

I met a Woman as I went walking;
We got talking,
Woman and I.
"Where are you going to, Woman, so early?"
(I said to the Woman as she went by).
"Down to the village to get some barley.
Will you come with me?" "No, not I."

I met some Rabbits as I went walking;
We got talking,
Rabbits and I.

"Where are you going in your brown fur coats?"
(I said to the Rabbits as they went by).
"Down to the village to get some oats.
Will you come with us?" "No, not I."

I met a Puppy as I went walking;
We got talking,
Puppy and I.
"Where are you going this nice fine day?"
(I said to the Puppy as he went by).
"Up in the hills to roll and play."
"*I'll* come with you, Puppy," said I.

A. A. MILNE

PETE AT THE ZOO

I wonder if the elephant
Is lonely in his stall
When all the boys and girls are gone
And there's no shout at all,
And there's no one to stamp before,
No one to note his might.
Does he hunch up, as I do,
Against the dark of night?

GWENDOLYN BROOKS

MY SHADOW

I have a little shadow that goes in and out with me,
But what can be the use of him is more than I can see.
He is very, very like me from the heels up to the head;
And I see him jump before me, when I jump into my bed.

The funniest thing about him is the way he likes to grow—
Not at all like proper children, which is always very slow;
For he sometimes shoots up taller like an india-rubber ball,
And he sometimes gets so little that there's none of him at all.

He hasn't got a notion of how children ought to play,
And can only make a fool of me in every sort of way.
He stays so close beside me, he's a coward you can see;
I'd think it shame to stick to nursie as that shadow sticks to me!

One morning, very early, before the sun was up,
I rose and found the shining dew on every buttercup;
But my lazy little shadow, like an arrant sleepy-head,
Had stayed at home beside me and was fast asleep in bed.

ROBERT LOUIS STEVENSON

THE QUESTION

People always say to me
"What do you think you'd like to be
When you grow up?"
And I say, "Why,
I think I'd like to be the sky
Or be a plane or train or mouse
Or maybe be a haunted house
Or something furry, rough and wild . . .
Or maybe I will stay a child."

KARLA KUSKIN

I looked in the mirror
And what did I see—
A funny little monkey
Looking back at me.

I looked in the kitchen
And what do you think—
I saw a swan swimming
In the kitchen sink.

I looked in the icebox
And what do you know—
Sitting on the cheese
Was a coal-black crow.

I looked in the bedroom
And under the bed—
I saw a little beetle
Stark stone dead.

I looked in the bathroom
And sitting in the tub—
Was a big polar bear
And her little bear cub.

I looked in the closet
And I had to laugh—
When I saw a long-necked
Spotty giraffe.

Wherever I looked
I found something queer—
A purple balloon
Or a blue reindeer,
A cat in the cupboard
A mouse in the tea—
But I never did find
What I went out to see.

No, I never did find
What I set out to see—
I looked everywhere
But I never found—*me*.

BEATRICE SCHENK DE REGNIERS

FLYING

I like to ride in my uncle's plane,
The one he pilots around the sky.
It's little and blue
And shiny, too,
And looks a lot like a dragonfly.

And once we're high in the summer air
With things below all shrunken in size,
It's easy to dream
How life would seem
If human beings were dragonflies.

The great wide river shrinks to a brook
That slowly winds away to the north,
Where ferries and tugs
Are water bugs
That skitter silently back and forth.

The faraway cows are just like ants,
The woods are patches of gray-green moss,
And telegraph lines
Where sunlight shines
Are glinting spider webs strung across.

It's quite exciting to hum through space
And view the world with an insect's eye.
A dragonfly-view
Makes things seem new,
Unless, of course, you're a dragonfly.

KAYE STARBIRD

LEAVETAKING

Vacation is over;
It's time to depart.
I must leave behind
(although it breaks my heart)

Tadpoles in the pond,
A can of eels,
A leaky rowboat,
Abandoned car wheels;

For I'm packing only
Necessities:
A month of sunsets
And two apple trees.

EVE MERRIAM

LITTLE DONKEY CLOSE YOUR EYES

Little Donkey on the hill
Standing there so very still
Making faces at the skies
Little Donkey close your eyes.

Little Monkey in the tree
Swinging there so merrily
Throwing cocoanuts at the skies
Little Monkey close your eyes.

Silly Sheep that slowly crop
Night has come and you must stop
Chewing grass beneath the skies
Silly Sheep now close your eyes.

Little Pig that squeals about
Make no noises with your snout
No more squealing to the skies
Little Pig now close your eyes.

Wild Young Birds that sweetly sing
Curve your heads beneath your wing
Dark night covers all the skies
Wild Young Birds now close your eyes.

Old Black Cat down in the barn
Keeping five small kittens warm
Let the wind blow in the skies
Dear Old Black Cat close your eyes.

Little Child all tucked in bed
Looking such a sleepy head
Stars are quiet in the skies
Little Child now close your eyes.

MARGARET WISE BROWN

GOING TO BED

I'm always told to hurry up—
  Which I'd be glad to do,
If there were not so many things
  That need attending to.

But first I have to find my towel
  Which fell behind the rack,
And when a pillow's thrown at me
  I have to throw it back.

And then I have to get the things
  I need in bed with me,
Like marbles and my birthday train
  And Pete the chimpanzee.

I have to see my polliwog
  Is safely in its pan,
And stand a minute on my head
  To be quite sure I can.

I have to bounce upon my bed
  To see if it will sink,
And then when I am covered up
  I find I need a drink.

MARCHETTE CHUTE

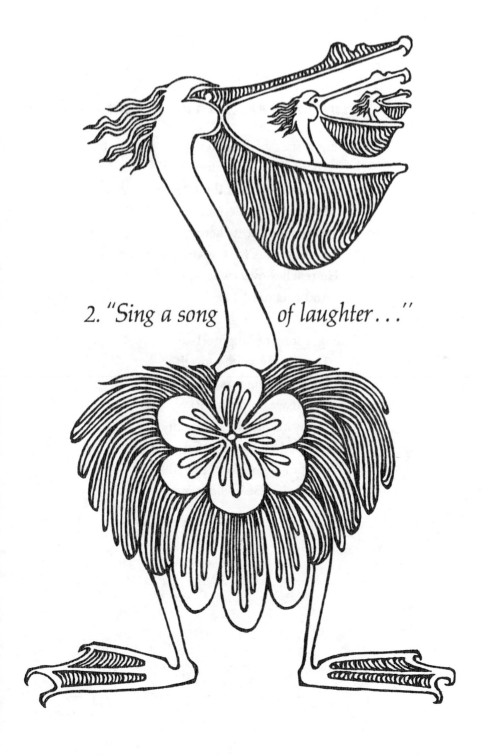

2. "Sing a song   of laughter..."

THE GIRAFFE AND THE WOMAN

Sing a song of laughter
　　About the young giraffter
Who tried to reach the rafter
　　To get the apple-pie;
The woman put it there, you know,
'Cause she was in despair, you know,
"He reaches everywhere, you know,
　　And eats until I *cry!*"

Sing a song of laughter!
　　The greedy young giraffter,
He got what he was after,
　　And it was piping hot!
It burnt his mouth so terribly,
He yelped and yammered yerribly,
The woman chuckled merrily,
　　And said, "See what you got!"

LAURA E. RICHARDS

ELETELEPHONY

Once there was an elephant,
Who tried to use the telephant—
No! no! I mean an elephone
Who tried to use the telephone—
(Dear me! I am not certain quite
That even now I've got it right.)

Howe'er it was, he got his trunk
Entangled in the telephunk;
The more he tried to get it free,
The louder buzzed the telephee—
(I fear I'd better drop the song
Of elephop and telephong!)

LAURA E. RICHARDS

DADDY FELL INTO THE POND

Everyone grumbled. The sky was grey.
We had nothing to do and nothing to say.
We were nearing the end of a dismal day,
And there seemed to be nothing beyond,
   THEN
   Daddy fell into the pond!

And everyone's face grew merry and bright,
And Timothy danced for sheer delight.
"Give me the camera, quick, oh quick!
He's crawling out of the duckweed." *Click!*

Then the gardener suddenly slapped his knee,
And doubled up, shaking silently,
And the ducks all quacked as if they were daft
And it sounded as if the old drake laughed.

O, there wasn't a thing that didn't respond
   WHEN
   Daddy fell into the pond!

ALFRED NOYES

MISS T.

It's a very odd thing—
   As odd as can be—
That whatever Miss T. eats
   Turns into Miss T.;
Porridge and apples,
   Mince, muffins and mutton,
Jam, junket, jumbles—
   Not a rap, not a button
It matters; the moment
   They're out of her plate,
Though shared by Miss Butcher
   And sour Mr. Bate;
Tiny and cheerful,
   And neat as can be,
Whatever Miss T. eats
   Turns into Miss T.

WALTER DE LA MARE

MUMMY SLEPT LATE
AND DADDY FIXED BREAKFAST

Daddy fixed breakfast.
He made us each a waffle.
It looked like gravel pudding.
It tasted something awful.

"Ha, ha," he said, "I'll try again.
This time I'll get it right."
But what *I* got was in between
Bituminous and anthracite.

"A little too well done? Oh well,
I'll have to start all over."
That time what landed on my plate
Looked like a manhole cover.

I tried to cut it with a fork:
The fork gave off a spark.
I tried a knife and twisted it
Into a question mark.

I tried it with a hack-saw.
I tried it with a torch.
It didn't even make a dent.
It didn't even scorch.

The next time Dad gets breakfast
When Mummy's sleeping late,
I think I'll skip the waffles.
I'd sooner eat the plate!

JOHN CIARDI

ANTONIO

Antonio, Antonio,
Was tired of living alonio.
   He thought he would woo
   Miss Lissamy Lou,
Miss Lissamy Lucy Molonio.

Antonio, Antonio,
Rode off on his polo-ponio.
   He found the fair maid
   In a bowery shade,
A-sitting and knitting alonio.

Antonio, Antonio,
Said, "If you will be my ownio
   I'll love you true,
   And I'll buy for you,
An icery creamery conio!"

"Oh, nonio, Antonio!
You're far too bleak and bonio!
   And all that I wish,
   You singular fish,
Is that you will quickly begonio."

Antonio, Antonio,
He uttered a dismal moanio;
   Then ran off and hid
   (Or I'm told that he did)
In the Antarctical Zonio.

LAURA E. RICHARDS

FATHER WILLIAM

"You are old, Father William," the young man said,
  "And your hair has become very white;
And yet you incessantly stand on your head—
  Do you think, at your age, it is right?"

"In my youth," Father William replied to his son,
  "I feared it might injure the brain;
But now that I'm perfectly sure I have none,
  Why, I do it again and again."

LEWIS CARROLL

SOME COOK!

Johnny made a custard
In the pepper pot.
Flavored it with mustard,
Put in quite a lot
Of garlic fried in olive oil,
Brought the custard to a boil,
Ate it up and burned his tongue—

You shouldn't cook when you're too young.

JOHN CIARDI

THE REASON FOR THE PELICAN

The reason for the pelican
Is difficult to see:
His beak is clearly larger
Than there's any need to be.

It's not to bail a boat with—
He doesn't own a boat.
Yet everywhere he takes himself
He has that beak to tote.

It's not to keep his wife in—
His wife has got one, too.
It's not a scoop for eating soup.
It's not an extra shoe.

It isn't quite for anything.
And yet you realize
It's really quite a splendid beak
In quite a splendid size.

JOHN CIARDI

BEWARE, MY CHILD

Beware, my child,
of the snaggle-toothed beast.
He sleeps till noon,
then makes his feast
on Hershey bars
and cakes of yeast
and anyone around—o.

So when you see him,
sneeze three times
and say three loud
and senseless rhymes
and give him all your
saved-up dimes,
or else you'll ne'er be found—o.

SHEL SILVERSTEIN

If you should meet a crocodile,
    Don't take a stick and poke him;
Ignore the welcome in his smile,
    Be careful not to stroke him.
For as he sleeps upon the Nile,
    He thinner gets and thinner;
And whene'er you meet a crocodile
    He's ready for his dinner.

AUTHOR UNKNOWN

DON'T EVER CROSS A CROCODILE

Don't ever cross a crocodile,
However few his faults.
Don't ever dare
A dancing bear
To teach you how to waltz.

Don't ever poke a rattlesnake
Who's sleeping in the sun
And say the poke
Was just a joke
And really all in fun.

Don't ever lure a lion close
With gifts of steak and suet.
Though lion-looks
Are nice in books
Don't ever, ever do it.

KAYE STARBIRD

GRIZZLY BEAR

If you ever, ever, ever meet a grizzly bear,
You must never, never, never ask him where
He is going,
Or what he is doing;
For if you ever, ever dare
To stop a grizzly bear,
You will never meet another grizzly bear.

MARY AUSTIN

ADVENTURES OF ISABEL

Isabel met an enormous bear,
Isabel, Isabel, didn't care.
The bear was hungry, the bear was ravenous,
The bear's big mouth was cruel and cavernous.
The bear said, Isabel, glad to meet you,
How do, Isabel, now I'll eat you!
Isabel, Isabel, didn't worry;
Isabel didn't scream or scurry.
She washed her hands and she straightened her hair up,
Then Isabel quietly ate the bear up.

OGDEN NASH

THE PURPLE COW

I never saw a Purple Cow,
I never hope to see one;
But I can tell you, anyhow,
I'd rather see than be one.

GELETT BURGESS

A WEE LITTLE WORM

A wee little worm in a hickory-nut
Sang, happy as he could be,
"O I live in the heart of the whole round world,
And it all belongs to me!"

JAMES WHITCOMB RILEY

There was an old man of Blackheath,
Who sat on his set of false teeth.
   Said he, with a start,
   "Oh, Lord, bless my heart!
I've bitten myself underneath!"

I raised a great hullabaloo
When I found a large mouse in my stew,
   Said the waiter, "Don't shout
   And wave it about,
Or the rest will be wanting one, too!"

There was a young lady of Ryde
Who ate a green apple and died.
   The apple fermented
   Within the lamented
And made cider inside her inside.

There was a young lady of Niger
Who smiled as she rode on a tiger;
    They returned from the ride
    With the lady inside,
And the smile on the face of the tiger.

AUTHOR UNKNOWN

There was an old man from Peru
Who dreamed he was eating his shoe;
    He woke in a fright
    In the middle of the night
And found it was perfectly true.

AUTHOR UNKNOWN

There was an Old Man with a beard,
Who said, "It is just as I feared!—
    Two Owls and a Hen,
    Two Larks and a Wren,
Have all built their nests in my beard!"

EDWARD LEAR

CATCH A LITTLE RHYME

Once upon a time
I caught a little rhyme

I set it on the floor
but it ran right out the door

I chased it on my bicycle
but it melted to an icicle

I scooped it up in my hat
but it turned into a cat

I caught it by the tail
but it stretched into a whale

I followed it in a boat
but it changed into a goat

When I fed it tin and paper
it became a tall skyscraper

Then it grew into a kite
and flew far out of sight . . .

EVE MERRIAM

3. "I like it when it's mizzly
and just a little drizzly . . ."

I LIKE IT WHEN IT'S MIZZLY

I like it when it's mizzly
and just a little drizzly
so everything looks far away
and make-believe and frizzly.

I like it when it's foggy
and sounding very froggy.
I even like it when it rains
on streets and weepy windowpanes
and catkins in the poplar tree
and *me*.

AILEEN FISHER

THE SOUNDING FOG

The fog comes in with a big sound
Made of small sounds from all around;

I hear the beat of sea-gulls' wings—
The storm wind as it sighs and sings—

I hear the clanging buoy-bell—
And dangers that the fog-horns tell

And every farthest sound of waves
Fog gathers—and it brings—and saves:

The gray fog hides away the Sea
Then brings it in a roar to me!

SUSAN NICHOLS PULSIFER

SUMMER RAIN

A shower, a sprinkle,
A tangle, a tinkle,
Greensilver runs the rain.

Like salt on your nose,
Like stars on your toes,
Tingles the tangy rain.

A tickle, a trickle,
A million-dot freckle
Speckles the spotted rain.

Like a cinnamon
Geranium
Smells the rainingest rain!

EVE MERRIAM

The dark gray clouds,
the great gray clouds,
the black rolling clouds are elephants
going down to the sea for water.
They draw up the water in their trunks.
They march back again across the sky.
They spray the earth again with the water,
and men say it is raining.

NATALIA M. BELTING

RAIN

Rain hits over and over
on hot tin,
on trucks,
on wires and roses.
Rain hits apples, birds, people,
coming in strokes of white,
gray, sometimes purple.
Rain cracks against my eyelids,
runs blue on my fingers,
and my shadow floats on the sidewalk
through trees and houses.

ADRIEN STOUTENBURG

APRIL RAIN SONG

Let the rain kiss you.
Let the rain beat upon your head with silver liquid drops.
Let the rain sing you a lullaby.

The rain makes still pools on the sidewalk.
The rain makes running pools in the gutter.
The rain plays a little sleep-song on our roof at night—

And I love the rain.

LANGSTON HUGHES

ON A SNOWY DAY

Fence posts wear marshmallow hats
On a winter's day,

Bushes in their nightgowns
Are kneeling down to pray,

And trees spread out their snowy skirts
Before they dance away.

DOROTHY ALDIS

SNOWFLAKES

I once thought that snowflakes were feathers
  And that they came falling down
When the Moon Lady feathered her chickens
  And shook out her silver gown.

And then I began to look closer,
  And now I know just what they are—
I caught one today in my mitten,
  And there was a baby star.

MARCHETTE CHUTE

SNOW IN SPRING

Feather on feather
on feather it falls,
white on the chimney pots,
rooftops and walls,
soft on the mountainside,
bright on the tree—
goose-feather snowflakes
all lovely and free;
I held seven snowflakes
with my hands . . . loose!
(oh! softer than swansdown
or feather-of-goose;
oh, brighter than starlight
or flower-of-May)—
but they were so magic
they melted away!

IVY O. EASTWICK

SNOW TOWARD EVENING

Suddenly the sky turned gray,
The day,
Which had been bitter and chill,
Grew intensely soft and still.
Quietly
From some invisible blossoming tree
Millions of petals cool and white
Drifted and blew,
Lifted and flew,
Fell with the falling night.

MELVILLE CANE

BLOW THE STARS HOME

Blow the Stars home, Wind, blow the Stars home
Ere Morning drowns them in golden foam.

ELEANOR FARJEON

Who has seen the wind?
    Neither I nor you:
But when the leaves hang trembling,
    The wind is passing through.

Who has seen the wind?
    Neither you nor I:
But when the leaves bow down their heads,
    The wind is passing by.

CHRISTINA ROSSETTI

THE WIND

I saw the wind to-day;
I saw it in the pane
Of glass upon the wall;
A moving thing—'twas like
No bird with widening wing,
No mouse that runs along
The meal-bag under the beam.

I think it like a horse,
All black, with frightening mane,
That springs out of the earth,
And tramples on his way.
I saw it in the glass,
The shaking of a mane
A horse that no one rides.

PADRAIC COLUM

I'll tell you how the sun rose,
A ribbon at a time.
The steeples swam in amethyst,
The news like squirrels ran.

The hills untied their bonnets,
The bobolinks begun.
Then I said softly to myself,
"That must have been the sun!"

But how he set, I know not.
There seemed a purple stile
Which little yellow boys and girls
Were climbing all the while

Till when they reached the other side,
A dominie in gray
Put gently up the evening bars,
And led the flock away.

EMILY DICKINSON

DAYBREAK

Daybreak comes first
   in thin splinters shimmering.
Neither is the day here
   nor is the night gone.
Night is getting ready to go
And Day whispers, "Soon now, soon."

CARL SANDBURG

A SUMMER MORNING

I saw dawn creep across the sky,
And all the gulls go flying by.
I saw the sea put on its dress
Of blue mid-summer loveliness.
And heard the trees begin to stir
Great arms of pine and juniper.
I heard the wind call out and say:
"Get up, my dear, it is to-day!"

RACHEL FIELD

VERY EARLY

When I wake in the early mist
The sun has hardly shown
And everything is still asleep
And I'm awake alone.
The stars are faint and flickering.
The sun is new and shy.
And all the world sleeps quietly,
Except the sun and I.
And then beginning noises start,
The whirrs and huffs and hums,
The birds peep out to find a worm,
The mice squeak out for crumbs,
The calf moos out to find the cow,
And taste the morning air
And everything is wide awake
And running everywhere.
The dew has dried,
The fields are warm,
The day is loud and bright,
And I'm the one who woke the sun
And kissed the stars good night.

KARLA KUSKIN

Some say the sun is a golden earring,
the earring of a beautiful girl.

A white bird took it from her
when she walked in the fields one day.
But it caught on a spider web
that stretches between the homes of men
and the homes of the gods.

NATALIA M. BELTING

4. "I saw a star slide down the sky . . ."

THE FALLING STAR

I saw a star slide down the sky,
Blinding the north as it went by,
Too burning and too quick to hold,
Too lovely to be bought or sold,
Good only to make wishes on
And then forever to be gone.

SARA TEASDALE

FEBRUARY TWILIGHT

I stood beside a hill
   Smooth with new-laid snow,
A single star looked out
   From the cold evening glow.

There was no other creature
   That saw what I could see—
I stood and watched the evening star
   As long as it watched me.

SARA TEASDALE

FULL OF THE MOON

It's full of the moon
The dogs dance out
Through brush and bush and bramble.
They howl and yowl
And growl and prowl.
They amble, ramble, scramble.
They rush through brush.
They push through bush.
They yip and yap and hurr.
They lark around and bark around
With prickles in their fur.
They two-step in the meadow.
They polka on the lawn.
Tonight's the night
The dogs dance out
And chase their tails till dawn.

KARLA KUSKIN

THE NIGHT

The night
   creeps in
   around my head
   and snuggles down
   upon the bed,
   and makes lace pictures
   on the wall
   but doesn't say a word at all.

MYRA COHN LIVINGSTON

THE MOON'S THE NORTH WIND'S COOKY

The moon's the North Wind's cooky.
He bites it, day by day,
Until there's but a rim of scraps
That crumble all away.

The South Wind is a baker.
He kneads clouds in his den,
And bakes a crisp new moon *that . . . greedy
North . . . Wind . . . eats . . . again!*

VACHEL LINDSAY

YET GENTLE WILL THE GRIFFIN BE

(What Grandpa Told the Children)

The moon? It is a griffin's egg,
Hatching to-morrow night.
And how the little boys will watch
With shouting and delight
To see him break the shell and stretch
And creep across the sky.
The boys will laugh. The little girls,
I fear, may hide and cry.
Yet gentle will the griffin be,
Most decorous and fat,
And walk up to the Milky Way
And lap it like a cat.

VACHEL LINDSAY

NIGHT

Night is a purple pumpkin,
Laced with a silver web,
And the moon a golden spider,
Wandering through the strands.
At dawn the purple pumpkin,
Rolling slowly around,
Leans against the star-web,
Moving the spider down.
The silver web slides slowly,
Slowly across the sky,
And the spider moon creeps slowly,
Slowly by.
The twinkling stars cease spinning
Their skeins of silver gray,
The spider moon
Crawls down the strands
And night turns into day.

PATRICIA HUBBELL

AUCTIONEER

Now I go down here and bring up a moon.
How much am I bid for the moon?
You see it a bright moon and brand-new.
What can I get to start it? how much?
What! who ever ever heard such a bid for a moon?
    Come now, gentlemen, come.
This is a solid guaranteed moon.
You may never have another chance
    to make a bid on such a compact
    eighteen-carat durable gold moon.
You could shape a thousand wedding rings
    out of this moongold.
I can guarantee the gold and the weddings
    will last forever
    and then a thousand years more.
Come, gentlemen, no nonsense, make me a bid.

CARL SANDBURG

THE PINWHEEL'S SONG

Seven around the moon go up
  (Light the fuse and away we go)
Two in silver and two in red
And two in blue, and one went dead.
  Six around the moon.

Six around the moon go up,
  Six around the moon.
Whirl in silver, whirl in blue,
Sparkle in red, and one burned through.
  Five around the moon.

Five around the moon go up
  (Rocketing up to the moon)
Sparkle and shine in a wonderful flare,
Till one went dead a mile in the air.
  Four around the moon.

Four to rocket around the moon.
  (Look at the crowds below!)
Four gone zooming above the sea,
But one got lost, and that makes three.
  Three around the moon.

Three around the moon go up.
   (Don't bump into a star!)
Silver and Red and whistling loud,
But Blue crashed into a thundercloud.
   Two around the moon.

Two around the moon, well, well.
   Two to reach the moon.
But Silver turned left, and Red turned right,
And CRASH! they splattered all over the night
   Falling away from the moon.

None of them going as far as the moon?
   None of them going that far?
Quick! Somebody light me another fuse.
But I'm all burned out . . . it's just no use. . . .
   It's really
      too far
        to
          the
            moo. . . .

JOHN CIARDI

NIGHT PLANE

The midnight plane with its riding lights
looks like a footloose star
wandering west through the blue-black night
to where the mountains are,
a star that's journeyed nearer earth
to tell each quiet farm
and little town, "Put out your lights,
children of earth. Sleep warm."

FRANCES FROST

ACQUAINTED WITH THE NIGHT

I have been one acquainted with the night.
I have walked out in rain—and back in rain.
I have outwalked the furthest city light.

I have looked down the saddest city lane.
I have passed by the watchman on his beat
And dropped my eyes, unwilling to explain.

I have stood still and stopped the sound of feet
When far away an interrupted cry
Came over houses from another street,

But not to call me back or say good-by;
And further still at an unearthly height,
One luminary clock against the sky

Proclaimed the time was neither wrong nor right.
I have been one acquainted with the night.

ROBERT FROST

LAST SONG

To the Sun
Who has shone
  All day,
To the Moon
Who has gone
  Away,
To the milk-white,
Silk-white,
Lily-white Star
A fond goodnight
Wherever you are.

JAMES GUTHRIE

5. "I saw
   a spooky witch
   out riding on her broom."

OCTOBER MAGIC

I know
I saw
  a spooky witch
  out riding on her broom.
I know
I saw
  a goblin thing
  who's laughing in my room.

I think
  perhaps I saw a ghost
  who had a pumpkin face,
  and creepy cats
  and sleepy bats
  are hiding every place.

  It doesn't matter where I look
  There's something to be seen,

  I know it is October
  So I think it's Halloween.

MYRA COHN LIVINGSTON

HALLOWE'EN

Tonight is the night
When dead leaves fly
Like witches on switches
Across the sky,
When elf and sprite
Flit through the night
On a moony sheen.

Tonight is the night
When leaves make a sound
Like a gnome in his home
Under the ground,
When spooks and trolls
Creep out of holes
Mossy and green.

Tonight is the night
When pumpkins stare
Through sheaves and leaves
Everywhere,
When ghoul and ghost
And goblin host
Dance round their queen.
It's Hallowe'en!

HARRY BEHN

If the moon shines
On the black pines
And an owl fl.es
And a ghost cries
And the hairs rise
On the back
  on the back
    on the back of your neck—

If you look quick
At the moon-slick
On the black air
And what goes there
Rides a broom-stick
And if things pick
At the back
  at the back
    at the back of your neck—

Would you know then
By the small men
With the lit grins
And with no chins,
By the owl's *hoo,*
And the ghost's *boo,*
By the Tom Cat,
And the Black Bat
On the night air,

And the thing there,
By the thing,
   by the thing,
      by the dark thing there

(Yes, you do,
   yes, you do
      know the thing I mean)

That it's now,
   that it's now,
      that it's—Halloween!

JOHN CIARDI

THE PUMPKIN

You may not believe it, for hardly could I:
I was cutting a pumpkin to put in a pie,
And on it was written in letters most plain
"You may hack me in slices, but I'll grow again."

I seized it and sliced it and made no mistake
As, with dough rounded over, I put it to bake:
But soon in the garden as I chanced to walk,
Why, there was that pumpkin entire on his stalk!

ROBERT GRAVES

THE WITCHES' RIDE

Over the hills
Where the edge of the light
Deepens and darkens
To ebony night,
Narrow hats high
Above yellow bead eyes,
The tatter-haired witches
Ride through the skies.
Over the seas
Where the flat fishes sleep
Wrapped in the slap of the slippery deep,
Over the peaks
Where the black trees are bare,
Where boney birds quiver
They glide through the air.
Silently humming
A horrible tune,
They sweep through the stillness
To sit on the moon.

KARLA KUSKIN

WAS SHE A WITCH?

There was an old woman
   Lived down in a dell;
She used to draw picklejacks
   Out of the well.
How did she do it?
Nobody knew it,
   She never, no never, no never would tell.

LAURA E. RICHARDS

THE LONELY SCARECROW

My poor old bones—I've only two—
A broomshank and a broken stave.
My ragged gloves are a disgrace.
My one peg-foot is in the grave.

I wear the labourer's old clothes:
Coat, shirt, and trousers all undone.
I bear my cross upon a hill
In rain and shine, in snow and sun.

I cannot help the way I look.
My funny hat is full of hay.
—O, wild birds, come and nest in me!
Why do you always fly away?

JAMES KIRKUP

THE GNOME

I saw a gnome
As plain as plain
Sitting on top
Of a weathervane.

He was dressed like a crow
In silky black feathers,
And there he sat watching
All kinds of weathers.

He talked like a crow too,
Caw caw caw,
When he told me exactly
What he saw,

Snow to the north of him
Sun to the south,
And he spoke with a beaky
Kind of a mouth.

But he wasn't a crow,
That was as plain as plain
'Cause crows never sit
On a weathervane.

What I saw was simply
A usual gnome
Looking things over
On his way home.

HARRY BEHN

MR. PYME

Once upon a time
Old Mr. Pyme
Lived all alone
Under a stone.

When the rain fell
He rang a bell,
When the sun shined
He laughed and dined

And floated to town
On thistledown,
And what a nice time
Had Mr. Pyme!

HARRY BEHN

SOME ONE

Some one came knocking
   At my wee, small door;
Some one came knocking,
   I'm sure—sure—sure;
I listened, I opened,
   I looked to left and right,
But nought there was a-stirring
   In the still dark night;
Only the busy beetle
   Tap-tapping in the wall,
Only from the forest
   The screech-owl's call,
Only the cricket whistling
   While the dewdrops fall,
So I know not who came knocking,
   At all, at all, at all.

WALTER DE LA MARE

YESTERDAY IN OXFORD STREET

Yesterday in Oxford Street, oh, what d'you think, my dears?
I had the most exciting time I've had for years and years;
The buildings looked so straight and tall, the sky was blue be-
    tween,
And, riding on a motor-bus, I saw the fairy queen!

Sitting there upon the rail and bobbing up and down,
The sun was shining on her wings and on her golden crown;
And looking at the shops she was, the pretty silks and lace—
She seemed to think that Oxford Sreet was quite a lovely place.

And once she turned and looked at me, and waved her little
    hand;
But I could only stare and stare—oh, would she understand?
I simply couldn't speak at all, I simply couldn't stir,
And all the rest of Oxford Street was just a shining blur.

Then suddenly she shook her wings—a bird had fluttered by—
And down into the street she looked and up into the sky;
And perching on the railing on a tiny fairy toe,
She flashed away so quickly that I hardly saw her go.

I never saw her any more, altho' I looked all day:
Perhaps she only came to peep, and never meant to stay:
But oh, my dears, just think of it, just think what luck for me,
That she should come to Oxford Street, and I be there to see!

ROSE FYLEMAN

Up the airy mountain,
  Down the rushy glen,
We daren't go a-hunting
  For fear of little men;
Wee folk, good folk,
  Trooping all together;
Green jacket, red cap,
  And white owl's feather!

Down along the rocky shore
  Some make their home—
They live on crispy pancakes
  Of yellow tide-foam;
Some in the reeds
  Of the black mountain lake,
With frogs for their watch-dogs,
  All night awake.

By the craggy hill-side,
  Through the mosses bare,
They have planted thorn-trees
  For pleasure here and there.
Is any man so daring
  As dig one up in spite,
He shall find their sharpest thorns
  In his bed at night.

Up the airy mountain,
　　Down the rushy glen,
We daren't go a-hunting
　　For fear of little men;
Wee folk, good folk,
　　Trooping all together;
Green jacket, red cap,
　　And white owl's feather!

WILLIAM ALLINGHAM

THE LITTLE ELF

I met a little Elfman once,
　　Down where the lilies blow.
I asked him why he was so small,
　　And why he didn't grow.

He slightly frowned, and with his eye
　　He looked me through and through—
"I'm quite as big for me," said he,
　　"As you are big for you!"

JOHN KENDRICK BANGS

I keep three wishes ready,
Lest I should chance to meet,
Any day a fairy
Coming down the street.

I'd hate to have to stammer,
Or have to think them out,
For it's very hard to think things up
When a fairy is about.

And I'd hate to lose my wishes,
For fairies fly away,
And perhaps I'd never have a chance
On any other day.

So I keep three wishes ready,
Lest I should chance to meet,
Any day a fairy
Coming down the street.

ANNETTE WYNNE

I'D LOVE TO BE A FAIRY'S CHILD

Children born of fairy stock
Never need for shirt or frock,
Never want for food or fire,
Always get their heart's desire:
Jingle pockets full of gold,
Marry when they're seven years old.
Every fairy child may keep
Two strong ponies and ten sheep;
All have houses, each his own,
Built of brick or granite stone;
They live on cherries, they run wild—
I'd love to be a fairy's child.

ROBERT GRAVES

ARIEL'S SONG

Where the bee sucks, there suck I.
In a cowslip's bell I lie;
There I couch when owls do cry.
On the bat's back I do fly ·
After summer merrily.
   Merrily, merrily, shall I live now
   Under the blossom that hangs on the bough.

WILLIAM SHAKESPEARE

6. "I wonder what the spring will shout . . ."

MARCH

A blue day,
a blue jay,
and a good beginning.

One crow,
melting snow—
spring's winning!

ELIZABETH COATSWORTH

For, lo, the winter is past,
The rain is over and gone;
The flowers appear on the earth;
The time of the singing of birds is come,
And the voice of the turtle is heard in our land.

THE BIBLE

APRIL

The roofs are shining from the rain,
  The sparrows twitter as they fly,
And with a windy April grace
  The little clouds go by.

Yet the back-yards are bare and brown
  With only one unchanging tree—
I could not be sure of Spring
  Save that it sings in me.

SARA TEASDALE

PIPPA'S SONG

The year's at the spring
And the day's at the morn;
Morning's at seven;
The hillside's dew-pearled;
The lark's on the wing;
The snail's on the thorn:
God's in his heaven—
All's right with the world!

ROBERT BROWNING

EASTER

The air is like a butterfly
  With frail blue wings.
The happy earth looks at the sky
  And sings.

JOYCE KILMER

JUNE

The day is warm
and a breeze is blowing,
the sky is blue
and its eye is glowing,
and everything's new
and green and growing . . . .

My shoes are off
and my socks are showing . . . .

My socks are off. . . .

Do you know how I'm going?

BAREFOOT!

AILEEN FISHER

OCTOBER

The month is amber,
　Gold, and brown.
Blue ghosts of smoke
　Float through the town,

Great V's of geese
　Honk overhead,
And maples turn
　A fiery red.

Frost bites the lawn.
　The stars are slits
In a black cat's eye
　Before she spits.

At last, small witches,
　Goblins, hags,
And pirates armed
　With paper bags,

Their costumes hinged
　On safety pins,
Go haunt a night
　Of pumpkin grins.

JOHN UPDIKE

When milkweed blows in the pasture
And winds start spinning the leaves,
And out by the wall the cornstalks
Are neatened in packs called sheaves;
When apples bump on the roadway
And over the road and higher
The last of the birds, like clothespins,
Are clipped to the telegraph wire . . .

I suddenly think, "Horse-chestnuts!"
And, singing a song, I go
And find a tree in the meadow
Where millions of chestnuts grow;
And underneath in the grasses
I gather the nuts, and then
As soon as I've filled my pockets,
I sing along home again.

And singing and scuffing homeward
Each year through the drying clover,
I feel like a king with treasure,
Though—now that I think it over—
I don't *do* much with horse-chestnuts
Except to make sure I've shined them.
It's just that fall
Isn't fall at all
Until I go out and find them.

KAYE STARBIRD

AUTUMN

The clock is striking autumn at the apple vendor's fair,
And the fruit is hanging heavy on the bough,
Up among the branches a summer bee still sings,
But winter is a whisper in its wings.
For the clock is striking autumn at the apple vendor's fair,
And the apples that are hanging soon will fall,
And the white cocoon of winter
Weave around the bending trees,
And the apples will lie broken on the ground.

PATRICIA HUBBELL

LEAVES

The leaves fall
Like big pennies,
And the sidewalk catches them.

PAUL WALKER

Over the wintry
forest, winds howl in a rage
with no leaves to blow.

SOSEKI

PENCIL AND PAINT

Winter has a pencil
For pictures clear and neat,
She traces the black tree-tops
Upon a snowy sheet,
But autumn has a palette
And a painting-brush instead,
And daubs the leaves for pleasure
With yellow, brown, and red.

ELEANOR FARJEON

THE CHRISTMAS PRESENT

The fields are wrapped in silver snow,
Tied tight with grey stone walls,
While cardinals flutter in the drifts
Like cheery Christmas balls.
   I wonder what the spring will shout
   When she unwraps the box,
   And finds to her extreme delight,
   A toad, a mole, a fox?

PATRICIA HUBBELL

LONG, LONG AGO

Winds through the olive trees
    Softly did blow,
Round little Bethlehem
    Long, long ago.

Sheep on the hillside lay
    Whiter than snow;
Shepherds were watching them,
    Long, long ago.

Then from the happy sky,
    Angels bent low,
Singing their songs of joy,
    Long, long ago.

For in a manger bed,
    Cradled we know,
Christ came to Bethlehem,
    Long, long ago.

AUTHOR UNKNOWN

ON CHRISTMAS MORN

(Adapted from an old Spanish carol)

Shall I tell you who will come
   to Bethlehem on Christmas Morn,
Who will kneel them gently down
   before the Lord, new-born?

One small fish from the river
   with scales of red, red gold.
One wild bee from the heather,
   one grey lamb from the fold,
One ox from the high pasture,
   one black bull from the herd,
One goatling from the far hills,
   one white, white bird.

And many children, God give them grace—
bringing tall candles to light Mary's face.

Shall I tell you who will come
   to Bethelehem on Christmas Morn,
Who will kneel them gently down
   before the Lord, new-born?

RUTH SAWYER

This is the week when Christmas comes.

Let every pudding burst with plums,
And every tree bear dolls and drums,
  In the week when Christmas comes.

Let every hall have boughs of green,
With berries glowing in between,
  In the week when Christmas comes.

Let every doorstep have a song
Sounding the dark street along,
  In the week when Christmas comes.

Let every steeple ring a bell
With a joyful tale to tell,
  In the week when Christmas comes.

Let every night put forth a star
To show us where the heavens are,
  In the week when Christmas comes.

Let every stable have a lamb
Sleeping warm beside its dam,
  In the week when Christmas comes.

This is the week when Christmas comes.

ELEANOR FARJEON

JANUARY

The days are short,
  The sun a spark
Hung thin between
  The dark and dark.

Fat snowy footsteps
  Track the floor.
Milk bottles burst
  Outside the door.

The river is
  A frozen place
Held still beneath
  The trees of lace.

The sky is low.
  The wind is gray.
The radiator
  Purrs all day.

JOHN UPDIKE

7. "I chanced to meet . . ."

THE CLOWN

I like to see
The spotted clown
Throwing dishes
In the air.
When they've started
Coming down
He looks as though
He didn't care,
But catches each one
Perfectly,
Over and over,
Every time,
One and two and
One-two-three—
Like a pattern
Or a rhyme.

DOROTHY ALDIS

One misty, moisty morning,
  When cloudy was the weather,
I chanced to meet an old man,
  Clothed all in leather.
He began to compliment
  And I began to grin.
How do you do? And how do you do?
  And how do you do again?

AUTHOR UNKNOWN

LEWIS HAS A TRUMPET

A trumpet
A trumpet
Lewis has a trumpet
A bright one that's yellow
A loud proud horn.
He blows it in the evening
When the moon is newly rising
He blows it when it's raining
In the cold and misty morn
It honks and it whistles
It roars like a lion
It rumbles like a lion
With a wheezing huffing hum
His parents say it's awful
Oh really simply awful
But
Lewis says he loves it
It's such a handsome trumpet
And when he's through with trumpets
He's going to buy a drum.

KARLA KUSKIN

Ho, for the Pirate Don Durk of Dowdee!
He was as wicked as wicked could be,
But oh, he was perfectly gorgeous to see!
   The Pirate Don Durk of Dowdee.

His conscience, of course, was as black as a bat,
But he had a floppety plume on his hat
And when he went walking it jiggled—like that!
   The plume of the Pirate Dowdee.

His coat it was crimson and cut with a slash,
And often as ever he twirled his mustache
Deep down in the ocean the mermaids went splash,
   Because of Don Durk of Dowdee.

Moreover, Dowdee had a purple tattoo,
And stuck in his belt where he buckled it through
Were a dagger, a dirk and a squizzamaroo,
   For fierce was the Pirate Dowdee.

So fearful he was he would shoot at a puff,
And always at sea when the weather grew rough
He drank from a bottle and wrote on his cuff,
   Did Pirate Don Durk of Dowdee.

Oh, he had a cutlass that swung at his thigh
And he had a parrot called Pepperkin Pye,
And a zigzaggy scar at the end of his eye
   Had Pirate Don Durk of Dowdee.

He kept in a cavern, this buccaneer bold,
A curious chest that was covered with mould,
And all of his pockets were jingly with gold!
    Oh jing! went the gold of Dowdee.

His conscience, of course, it was crook'd like a squash,
But both of his boots made a slickery slosh,
And he went through the world with a wonderful swash,
    Did Pirate Don Durk of Dowdee.

It's true he was wicked as wicked could be,
His sins they outnumbered a hundred and three,
But oh, he was perfectly gorgeous to see,
    The Pirate Don Durk of Dowdee.

MILDRED PLEW MEIGS

Poor old Jonathan Bing
Went out in his carriage to visit the King,
But everyone pointed and said, "Look at that!
Jonathan Bing has forgotten his hat!"
(He'd forgotten his hat!)

Poor old Jonathan Bing
Went home and put on his hat for the King,
But up by the palace a soldier said, "Hi!
You can't see the King; you've forgotten your tie!"
(He'd forgotten his tie!)

Poor old Jonathan Bing,
He put on a *beautiful* tie for the King,
But when he arrived an Archbishop said, "No!
You can't come to court in pyjamas, you know!"

Poor old Jonathan Bing
Went home and addressed a short note to the King:
    If you please will excuse me
    I won't come to tea;
    For home's the best place for
    All people like me!

BEATRICE CURTIS BROWN

CATHERINE

Catherine said "I think I'll bake
A most delicious chocolate cake."
She took some mud and mixed it up
While adding water from a cup
And then some weeds and nuts and bark
And special gravel from the park
A thistle and a dash of sand.
She beat out all the lumps by hand.
And on the top she wrote "To You"
The way she says the bakers do
And then she signed it "Fondly C."
And gave the whole of it to me.
I thanked her but I wouldn't dream
Of eating cake without ice cream.

KARLA KUSKIN

EAT-IT-ALL ELAINE

I went away last August
To summer camp in Maine,
And there I met a camper
Called Eat-it-all Elaine.
Although Elaine was quiet,
She liked to cause a stir
By acting out the nickname
Her camp-mates gave to her.

The day of our arrival
At Cabin Number Three
When girls kept coming over
To greet Elaine and me,
She took a piece of Kleenex
And calmly chewed it up,
Then strolled outside the cabin
And ate a buttercup.

Elaine, from that day forward,
Was always in command.
On hikes, she'd eat some birch-bark
On swims, she'd eat some sand.
At meals, she'd swallow prune-pits
And never have a pain,
While everyone around her
Would giggle, "Oh, Elaine!"

One morning, berry-picking,
A bug was in her pail,
And though we thought for certain
Her appetite would fail,
Elaine said, "Hmm, a stinkbug."
And while we murmured, "Ooh,"
She ate her pail of berries
And ate the stinkbug, too.

The night of Final Banquet
When counselors were handing
Awards to different children
Whom they believed outstanding,
To every *thinking* person
At summer camp in Maine
The Most Outstanding Camper
Was Eat-it-all Elaine.

KAYE STARBIRD

Before she has her floor swept
  Or her dishes done,
Any day you'll find her
  A-sunning in the sun!

It's long after midnight
  Her key's in the lock,
And you never see her chimney smoke
  Till past ten o'clock!

She digs in her garden
  With a shovel and a spoon,
She weeds her lazy lettuce
  By the light of the moon.

She walks up the walk
  Like a woman in a dream,
She forgets she borrowed butter
  And pays you back cream!

Her lawn looks like a meadow,
  And if she mows the place
She leaves the clover standing
  And the Queen Anne's lace!

EDNA ST. VINCENT MILLAY

These buildings are too close to me.
I'd like to PUSH away.
I'd like to live in the country,
And spread my arms all day.

I'd like to spread my breath out, too—
As farmers' sons and daughters do.

I'd tend the cows and chickens.
I'd do the other chores.
Then, all the hours left I'd go
A-SPREADING out-of-doors.

GWENDOLYN BROOKS

OTTO

It's Christmas Day. I did not get
The presents that I hoped for. Yet,
It is not nice to frown or fret.

To frown or fret would not be fair.
My Dad must never know I care
It's hard enough for him to bear.

GWENDOLYN BROOKS

CALIBAN IN THE COAL MINES

God, we don't like to complain;
  We know that the mine is no lark.
But—there's the pools from the rain;
  But—there's the cold and the dark.

God, You don't know what it is—
  You, in Your well-lighted sky—
Watching the meteors whizz,
  Warm, with a sun always by.

God, if You had but the moon
  Stuck in Your cap for a lamp,
Even You'd tire of it soon,
  Down in the dark and the damp.

Nothing but blackness above
  And nothing that moves but the cars . . .
God, if You wish for our love,
  Fling us a handful of stars!

LOUIS UNTERMEYER

I hear America singing, the varied carols I hear,

Those of the mechanics, each singing his as it should be blithe
and strong,

The carpenter singing his as he measures his plank or beam,

The mason singing his as he makes ready for work or leaves off
work,

The boatman singing what belongs to him in his boat, the deck
hand singing on the steamboat deck,

The shoemaker singing as he sits on his bench, the hatter singing as he stands,

The wood-cutter's song, the ploughboy's on his way in the
morning, or at noon intermission or at sundown,

The delicious singing of the mother, or the young wife at work,
or the girl sewing or washing,

Each sings what belongs to him or her and to none else,

The day what belongs to the day—at night the party of young
fellows, robust, friendly,

Singing with open mouths their strong melodious songs.

WALT WHITMAN

SOME PEOPLE

Isn't it strange some people make
   You feel so tired inside,
Your thoughts begin to shrivel up
   Like leaves all brown and dried!

But when you're with some other ones,
   It's stranger still to find
Your thoughts as thick as fireflies
   All shiny in your mind!

RACHEL FIELD

8. "I'd take the hound with the drooping ears . . ."

THE ANIMAL STORE

If I had a hundred dollars to spend,
  Or maybe a little more,
I'd hurry as fast as my legs would go
  Straight to the animal store.

I wouldn't say, "How much for this or that?"
  "What kind of a dog is he?"
I'd buy as many as rolled an eye,
  Or wagged a tail at me!

I'd take the hound with the drooping ears
  That sits by himself alone;
Cockers and Cairns and wobbly pups
  For to be my very own.

I might buy a parrot all red and green,
  And the monkey I saw before,
If I had a hundred dollars to spend,
  Or maybe a little more.

RACHEL FIELD

MY DOG

His nose is short and scrubby;
  His ears hang rather low;
And he always brings the stick back,
  No matter how far you throw.

He gets spanked rather often
  For things he shouldn't do,
Like lying-on-beds, and barking,
  And eating up shoes when they're new.

He always wants to be going
  Where he isn't supposed to go.
He tracks up the house when it's snowing—
  Oh, puppy, I love you so.

MARCHETTE CHUTE

THE HAIRY DOG

My dog's so furry I've not seen
His face for years and years:
His eyes are buried out of sight,
I only guess his ears.

When people ask me for his breed,
I do not know or care:
He has the beauty of them all
Hidden beneath his hair.

HERBERT ASQUITH

LONE DOG

I'm a lean dog, a keen dog, a wild dog, and lone;
I'm a rough dog, a tough dog, hunting on my own!
I'm a bad dog, a mad dog, teasing silly sheep;
I love to sit and bay the moon, to keep fat souls from sleep.

I'll never be a lap dog, licking dirty feet,
A sleek dog, a meek dog, cringing for my meat,
Not for me the fireside, the well-filled plate,
But shut door, and sharp stone, and cuff and kick and hate.

Not for me the other dogs, running by my side,
Some have run a short while, but none of them would bide.
O mine is still the one trail, the hard trail, the best
Wide wind, and wild stars, and hunger of the quest!

IRENE RUTHERFORD MC LEOD

CATS

Cats sleep
Anywhere,
Any table,
Any chair,
Top of piano,
Window-ledge,
In the middle,
On the edge,
Open drawer,
Empty shoe,
Anybody's
Lap will do,
Fitted in a
Cardboard box,
In the cupboard
With your frocks—
Anywhere!
They don't care!
Cats sleep
Anywhere.

ELEANOR FARJEON

THE RUM TUM TUGGER

The Rum Tum Tugger is a Curious Cat;
If you offer him pheasant he would rather have grouse.
If you put him in a house he would much prefer a flat,
If you set him on a mouse then he only wants a rat,
If you set him on a rat then he'd rather chase a mouse,
Yes the Rum Tum Tugger is a Curious Cat—
> And there isn't any call for me to shout it:
>> For he will do
>> As he do do
>>> And there's no doing anything about it!

The Rum Tum Tugger is a terrible bore:
When you let him in, then he wants to be out;
He's always on the wrong side of every door,
As soon as he's at home, then he'd like to get about.
He likes to lie in the bureau drawer,
But he makes such a fuss if he can't get out.
Yes the Rum Tum Tugger is a Curious Cat—
> And it isn't any use for you to doubt it:
>> For he will do
>> As he do do
>>> And there's no doing anything about it!

The Rum Tum Tugger is a curious beast:
His disobliging ways are a matter of habit.
If you offer him fish then he always wants a feast;
When there isn't any fish then he won't eat rabbit.
If you offer him cream then he sniffs and sneers,
For he only likes what he finds for himself;
So you'll catch him in it right up to the ears,
If you put it away on the larder shelf.
The Rum Tum Tugger is artful and knowing,
The Rum Tum Tugger doesn't care for a cuddle;
But he'll leap on your lap in the middle of your sewing,
For there's nothing he enjoys like a horrible muddle.
Yes the Rum Tum Tugger is a Curious Cat—
    And there isn't any need for me to spout it:
    For he will do
    As he do do
    And there's no doing anything about it!

T. S. ELIOT

MOON

I have a white cat whose name is Moon;
He eats catfish from a wooden spoon,
And sleeps till five each afternoon.

Moon goes out when the moon is bright
And sycamore trees are spotted white
To sit and stare in the dead of night.

Beyond still water cries a loon,
Through mulberry leaves peers a wild baboon
And in Moon's eyes I see the moon.

WILLIAM JAY SMITH

THE PRAYER OF THE CAT

Lord,
I am the cat.
It is not, exactly, that I have something to ask of You!
No—
I ask nothing of anyone—
but,
if You have by some chance, in some celestial barn,
a little white mouse,
or a saucer of milk,
I know someone who would relish them.
Wouldn't You like someday
to put a curse on the whole race of dogs?
If so I should say,

Amen

CARMEN BERNOS DE GASZTOLD

POEM

As the cat
climbed over
the top of

the jamcloset
first the right
forefoot

carefully
then the hind
stepped down

into the pit of
the empty
flowerpot.

WILLIAM CARLOS WILLIAMS

MICE

I think mice
Are rather nice.

Their tails are long,
Their faces small,
They haven't any
Chins at all.
Their ears are pink,
Their teeth are white,
They run about
The house at night.
They nibble things
They shouldn't touch
And no one seems
To like them much.

But I think mice
Are nice.

ROSE FYLEMAN

MISSING

Has anybody seen my mouse?

I opened his box for half a minute,
Just to make sure he was really in it,
And while I was looking, he jumped outside!
I tried to catch him, I tried, I tried. . . .
I think he's somewhere about the house.
Has *anyone* seen my mouse?

Uncle John, have you seen my mouse?

Just a small sort of mouse, a dear little brown one,
He came from the country, he wasn't a town one,
So he'll feel all lonely in a London street;
Why, what could he possibly find to eat?

He must be somewhere. I'll ask Aunt Rose:
Have you seen a mouse with a woffelly nose?
Oh, somewhere about—
He's just got out. . . .

Hasn't anybody seen my mouse?

A. A. MILNE

THE MOUSE
IN THE WAINSCOT

Hush, Suzanne!
Don't lift your cup.
The breath you heard
Is a mouse getting up.

As the mist that steams
From your milk as you sup,
So soft is the sound
Of a mouse getting up.

There! did you hear
His feet pitter-patter,
Lighter than tipping
Of beads on a platter.

And then like a shower
On the window pane
The little feet scampering
Back again?

O falling of feather!
O drift of leaf!
The mouse in the wainscot
Is dropping asleep.

IAN SERRAILLIER

THE OLD WOMAN

You know the old woman
  Who lived in a shoe?
And had so many children
  She didn't know what to do?

I think if she lived in
  A little shoe-house—
That little old woman was
  Surely a mouse!

BEATRIX POTTER

BIRTHDAY CAKE

If little mice have birthdays
(and I suppose they do)

And have a family party
(and guests invited too)

And have a cake with candles
(it would be rather small)

I bet a birthday CHEESE cake
would please them most of all.

AILEEN FISHER

THE PRAYER OF THE MOUSE

I am so little and grey,
dear God,
how can You keep me in mind?
Always spied upon,
always chased.
Nobody ever gives me anything,
and I nibble meagrely at life.
Why do they reproach me with being a mouse?
Who made me but You?
I only ask to stay hidden.
Give me my hunger's pittance
safe from the claws
of that devil with green eyes.
                    Amen

CARMEN BERNOS DE GASZTOLD

THE LITTLE TURTLE

There was a little turtle.
He lived in a box.
He swam in a puddle.
He climbed on the rocks.

He snapped at a mosquito.
He snapped at a flea.
He snapped at a minnow.
And he snapped at me.

He caught the mosquito.
He caught the flea.
He caught the minnow.
But he didn't catch me.

VACHEL LINDSAY

THE PRAYER OF THE GOLDFISH

O God,
forever I turn in this hard crystal,
so transparent, yet I can find no way out.
Lord,
deliver me from the cramp of this water
and these terrifying things I see through it.
Put me back in the play of Your torrents,
in Your limpid springs.
Let me no longer be a little goldfish
in its prison of glass,
but a living spark
in the gentleness of Your reeds.

                                        Amen

CARMEN BERNOS DE GASZTOLD

FOAL

Come trotting up
Beside your mother,
Little skinny.

Lay your neck across
Her back, and whinny,
Little foal.

You think you're a horse
Because you can trot—
But you're not.

Your eyes are so wild,
And each leg is as tall
As a pole;

And you're only a skittish
Child, after all,
Little foal.

MARY BRITTON MILLER

WHITE HORSES

Count the white horses you meet on the way,
Count the white horses, child, day after day,
Keep a wish ready for wishing—if you
Wish on the ninth horse, your wish will come true.

I saw a white horse at the end of the lane,
I saw a white horse canter down by the shore,
I saw a white horse that was drawing a wain,
And one drinking out of a trough: that made four.

I saw a white horse gallop over the down,
I saw a white horse looking over a gate,
I saw a white horse on the way into town,
And one on the way coming back: that made eight.

But oh for the ninth one: where *he* tossed his mane,
And cantered and galloped and whinnied and swished
His silky white tail, I went looking in vain,
And the wish I had ready could never be wished.

Count the white horses you meet on the way,
Count the white horses, child, day after day,
Keep a wish ready for wishing—if you
Wish on the ninth horse, your wish will come true.

ELEANOR FARJEON

A gigantic beauty of a stallion, fresh and responsive to
    my caresses,
Head high in the forehead, wide between the ears,
Limbs glossy and supple, tail dusting the ground,
Eyes full of sparkling wickedness, ears finely cut,
    flexibly moving.

His nostrils dilate as my heels embrace him,
His well-built limbs tremble with pleasure as we race around
    and return.
I but use you a minute, then I resign you, stallion.
Why do I need your paces when I myself out-gallop them?
Even as I stand or sit passing faster than you.

WALT WHITMAN

Once when the snow of the year was beginning to fall,
We stopped by a mountain pasture to say, "Whose colt?"
A little Morgan had one forefoot on the wall,
The other curled at his breast. He dipped his head
And snorted at us. And then he had to bolt.
We heard the miniature thunder where he fled,
And we saw him, or thought we saw him, dim and gray,
Like a shadow against the curtain of falling flakes.
"I think the little fellow's afraid of the snow.
He isn't winter-broken. It isn't play
With the little fellow at all. He's running away.
I doubt if even his mother could tell him, 'Sakes,
It's only weather.' He'd think she didn't know!
Where is his mother? He can't be out alone."
And now he comes again with clatter of stone,
And mounts the wall again with whited eyes
And all his tail that isn't hair up straight.
He shudders his coat as if to throw off flies.
"Whoever it is that leaves him out so late,
When other creatures have gone to stall and bin,
Ought to be told to come and take him in."

ROBERT FROST

THE PRAYER OF THE OLD HORSE

See, Lord,
my coat hangs in tatters,
like homespun, old, threadbare.
All that I had of zest,
all my strength,
I have given in hard work
and kept nothing back for myself.
Now
my poor head swings
to offer up all the loneliness of my heart.
Dear God,
stiff on my thickened legs
I stand here before You:
Your unprofitable servant.
Oh! of Your goodness,
give me a gentle death.

Amen

CARMEN BERNOS DE GASZTOLD

9. "I heard   a bird sing . . ."

I heard a bird sing
  In the dark of December
A magical thing
  And sweet to remember.

"We are nearer to Spring
  Than we were in September,"
I heard a bird sing
  In the dark of December.

OLIVER HERFORD

A bird came down the walk:
He did not know I saw;
He bit an angle-worm in halves
And ate the fellow, raw.

And then he drank a dew
From a convenient grass,
And then hopped sidewise to the wall
To let a beetle pass.

EMILY DICKINSON

THE HENS

The night was coming very fast;
It reached the gate as I ran past.

The pigeons had gone to the tower of the church
And all the hens were on their perch,

Up in the barn, and I thought I heard
A piece of a little purring word.

I stopped inside, waiting and staying,
To try to hear what the hens were saying.

They were asking something, that was plain,
Asking it over and over again.

One of them moved and turned around,
Her feathers made a ruffled sound,

A ruffled sound, like a bushful of birds,
And she said her little asking words.

She pushed her head close into her wing,
But nothing answered anything.

ELIZABETH MADOX ROBERTS

All along the backwater,
Through the rushes tall,
Ducks are a-dabbling,
Up tails all!

Ducks' tails, drakes' tales,
Yellow feet a-quiver,
Yellow bills all out of sight
Busy in the river!

Slushy green undergrowth
Where the roach swim
Here we keep our larder,
Cool and full and dim.

Every one for what he likes!
We like to be
Heads down, tails up,
Dabbling free!

High in the blue above
Swifts whirl and call
We are down a-dabbling,
Up tails all.

KENNETH GRAHAME

THE PRAYER OF THE LITTLE DUCKS

Dear God,
give us a flood of water.
Let it rain tomorrow and always.
Give us plenty of little slugs
and other luscious things to eat.
Protect all folk who quack
and everyone who knows how to swim.

Amen

CARMEN BERNOS DE GASZTOLD

THE BIRD'S NEST

I know a place, in the ivy on a tree,
Where a bird's nest is, and the eggs are three,
And the bird is brown, and the eggs are blue,
And the twigs are old, but the moss is new,
And I go quite near, though I think I should have heard
The sound of me watching, if I had been a bird.

JOHN DRINKWATER

CROWS

I like to walk
And hear the black crows talk.

I like to lie
And watch crows sail the sky.

I like the crow
That wants the wind to blow:

I like the one
That thinks the wind is fun.

I like to see
Crows spilling from a tree,

And try to find
The top crow left behind.

I like to hear
Crows caw that spring is near.

I like the great
Wild clamor of crow hate

Three farms away
When owls are out by day.

I like the slow
Tired homeward-flying crow;

I like the sight
Of crows for my good night.

DAVID MCCORD

DUST OF SNOW

The way a crow
Shook down on me
The dust of snow
From a hemlock tree

Has given my heart
A change of mood
And saved some part
Of a day I had rued.

ROBERT FROST

THE EAGLE

He clasps the crag with crooked hands;
Close to the sun in lonely lands,
Ring'd with the azure world, he stands.

The wrinkled sea beneath him crawls;
He watches from his mountain walls,
And like a thunderbolt he falls.

ALFRED TENNYSON

THE OWL

The Owl that lives in the old oak tree
Opens his eyes and cannot see
When it's clear as day to you and me;
But not long after the sun goes down
And the Church Clock strikes in Tarrytown
And Nora puts on her green nightgown,
He opens his big bespectacled eyes
And shuffles out of the hollow tree,
And flies and flies
                    and flies and flies,
And flies and flies
                    and flies and flies.

WILLIAM JAY SMITH

Something told the wild geese
  It was time to go.
Though the fields lay golden
  Something whispered, "Snow."
Leaves were green and stirring
  Berries, luster-glossed,
But beneath warm feathers
  Something cautioned, "Frost."
All the sagging orchards
  Steamed with amber spice.
But each wild breast stiffened
  At remembered ice.
Something told the wild geese,
  It was time to fly—
Summer sun was on their wings,
  Winter in their cry.

RACHEL FIELD

The wild geese returning
Through the misty sky—
Behold they look like
A letter written
In faded ink!

TSUMORI KUNIMOTO

SEAGULLS

We have no time for bridges,
Those man-made spans that
Hang between desires,
One island joined to next
By steel and stone.
We leap from shore to shore
On wings of light and see
The bridges, traffic-choked,
Below;
Those shafts whose cruel
Impending ways turn even music
To a crawl.
We leap and fly and light
The winter sky with wings.
   Night soon descends
   And bridges disappear
   In dark.

PATRICIA HUBBELL

THE HERON

The heron stands in water where the swamp
Has deepened to the blackness of a pool,
Or balances with one leg on a hump
Of marsh grass heaped above a muskrat hole.

He walks the shallow with an antic grace.
The great feet break the ridges of the sand,
The long eye notes the minnow's hiding place.
His beak is quicker than a human hand.

He jerks a frog across his bony lip,
Then points his heavy bill above the wood.
The wide wings flap but once to lift him up.
A single ripple starts from where he stood.

THEODORE ROETHKE

PEOPLE BUY A LOT OF THINGS

People buy a lot of things—
Carts and balls and nails and rings,
But I would buy a bird that sings.

I would buy a bird that sings and let it sing for me,
And let it sing of flying things and mating in a tree,
And then I'd open wide the cage, and set the singer free.

ANNETTE WYNNE

STUPIDITY STREET

I saw with open eyes
Singing birds sweet
Sold in the shops
For the people to eat,
Sold in the shops of
Stupidity Street.

I saw in a vision
The worm in the wheat,
And in the shops nothing
For people to eat:
Nothing for sale in
Stupidity Street.

RALPH HODGSON

10. "I found new-born foxes ..."

Dear Father
hear and bless
thy beasts and
singing birds.
And guard with
tenderness
small things
that have
no words.

MARGARET WISE BROWN

TO A SQUIRREL
AT KYLE-NA-NO

Come play with me;
Why should you run
Through the shaking tree
As though I'd a gun
To strike you dead?
When all I would do
Is to scratch your head
And let you go.

W. B. YEATS

THE SQUIRREL

Whisky, frisky,
Hippity hop,
Up he goes
To the tree top!

Whirly, twirly,
Round and round,
Down he scampers
To the ground.

Furly, curly,
What a tail!
Tall as a feather,
Broad as a sail!

Where's his supper?
In the shell,
Snappity, crackity,
Out it fell!

AUTHOR UNKNOWN

In and out the bushes, up the ivy,
Into the hole
By the old oak stump, the chipmunk flashes
Up the pole.

To the feeder full of seeds he dashes,
Stuffs his cheeks,
The chickadee and titmouse scold him.
Down he streaks.

Red as the leaves the wind blows off the maple,
Red as a fox,
Striped like a skunk, the chipmunk whistles
Past the love seat, past the mailbox,

Down the path,
Home to his warm hole stuffed with sweet
Things to eat.
Neat and slight and shining, his front feet

Curled at his breast, he sits there while the sun
Stripes the red west
With its last light: the chipmunk
Dives to his rest.

RANDALL JARRELL

BEE SONG

Bees in the late summer sun
Drone their song
Of yellow moons
Trimming black velvet,
Droning, droning a sleepysong.

CARL SANDBURG

BUMBLE BEE

Black and yellow
Little fur bee
Buzzing away
In the timothy
Drowsy
Browsy
Lump of a bee
Rumbly
Tumbly
Bumbly bee.
Where are you taking
Your golden plunder
Humming along
Like baby thunder?
Over the clover
And over the hay
Then over the apple trees
Zoom away.

MARGARET WISE BROWN

FIREFLY

A Song

A little light is going by,
Is going up to see the sky,
A little light with wings.

I never could have thought of it,
To have a little bug all lit
And made to go on wings.

ELIZABETH MADOX ROBERTS

A DRAGON-FLY

When the heat of the summer
Made drowsy the land,
A dragon-fly came
And sat on my hand,
With its blue jointed body,
And wings like spun glass,
It lit on my fingers
As though they were grass.

ELEANOR FARJEON

WHITE BUTTERFLIES

Fly, white butterflies, out to sea,
Frail, pale wings for the wind to try,
Small white wings that we scarce can see,
      Fly!
Some fly light as a laugh of glee,
Some fly soft as a long, low sigh;
All to the haven where each would be.
      Fly!

    ALGERNON CHARLES SWINBURNE

CRICKETS

all busy punching tickets,
clicking their little punches.
The tickets come in bunches,
good for a brief excursion,
good for a cricket's version
of travel (before it snows) to
the places a cricket goes to.
Alas! the crickets sing alas
in the dry September grass.
Alas, alas, in every acre,
every one a ticket-taker.

    DAVID MC CORD

MRS. SPIDER

Mrs. Spider
  found a place
  where she could spin a house of lace;

  a room where she might entertain
  a gnat upon the windowpane,

  and windows, where a little fly
  might peep, and frightened, buzz right by.

MYRA COHN LIVINGSTON

OF A SPIDER

The spider weaves his silver wire
Between the cherry and the brier.

He runs along and sees the thread
Well-fastened on each hawser-head.

And then within his wheel he dozes
Hung on a thorny stem of roses,

While fairies ride the silver ferry
Between the rose-bud and the cherry.

WILFRID THORLEY

THE BAT

By day the bat is cousin to the mouse.
He likes the attic of an aging house.

His fingers make a hat about his head.
His pulse beat is so slow we think him dead.

He loops in crazy figures half the night
Among the trees that face the corner light.

But when he brushes up against a screen,
We are afraid of what our eyes have seen:

For something is amiss or out of place
When mice with wings can wear a human face.

THEODORE ROETHKE

THE JOLLY WOODCHUCK

The woodchuck's very very fat
But doesn't care a pin for that.

When nights are long and the snow is deep,
Down in his hole he lies asleep.

Under the earth is a warm little room
The drowsy woodchuck calls his home.

Rolls of fat and fur surround him,
With all his children curled around him.

Snout to snout and tail to tail.
He never awakes in the wildest gale;

When icicles snap and the north wind blows
He snores in his sleep and rubs his nose.

MARION EDEY *and* DOROTHY GRIDER

RACCOONS

Did you ever look
near a wildish brook
or a green-eyed pond
with a wood beyond
and see (on the bank
where the grass grows rank)
a five-toed track?
Hands in front
and feet in back
like an all-four child
in a place so wild?
There a raccoon
on a late afternoon
or under the light
of a lantern moon
went looking for frogs
and mice to eat . . .
in his barefoot feet.
That's where he walked
in the thick black ooze
without any shoes.

And so will I
when the sun is high
in the wide June sky!

AILEEN FISHER

FOUR LITTLE FOXES

Speak gently, Spring, and make no sudden sound;
For in my windy valley, yesterday, I found
New-born foxes squirming on the ground—
                Speak gently.

Walk softly, March, forbear the bitter blow;
Her feet within a trap, her blood upon the snow,
The four little foxes saw their mother go—
                Walk softly.

Go lightly, Spring, oh, give them no alarm;
When I covered them with boughs to shelter them from harm,
The thin blue foxes suckled at my arm—
                Go lightly.

Step softly, March, with your rampant hurricane;
Nuzzling one another, and whimpering with pain,
The new little foxes are shivering in the rain—
                Step softly.

LEW SARETT

THE SNARE

I hear a sudden cry of pain!
   There is a rabbit in a snare;
Now I hear the cry again,
   But I cannot tell from where.

But I cannot tell from where
   He is calling out for aid;
Crying on the frightened air,
   Making everything afraid.

Making everything afraid,
   Wrinkling up his little face,
As he cries again for aid;
   And I cannot find the place!

And I cannot find the place
   Where his paw is in the snare:
Little one! Oh, little one!
   I am searching everywhere!

JAMES STEPHENS

All but blind
  In his chambered hole
Gropes for worms
  The four-clawed Mole.

All but blind
  In the evening sky
The hooded Bat
  Twirls softly by.

All but blind
  In the burning day
The Barn Owl blunders
  On her way.

And blind as are
  These three to me,
So, blind to Some One
  I must be.

WALTER DE LA MARE

God, keep all claw-denned alligators
Free.
Keep snake and lizard, tortoise, toad,
All creep-crawl
Tip-toe turtles
Where they stand,
Keep these;
All smile-mouthed crocodiles,
Young taut-skinned, sun-wet
Creatures of the sea,
Thin, indecisive hoppers
Of the shore,
Keep these;
All hurt, haunt, hungry
Reptiles
Wandering the marge,
All land-confused
Amphibians,
Sea-driven,
Keep these;
Keep snakes, toads, lizards,
All hop, all crawl, all climb,
Keep these,
Keep these.

PATRICIA HUBBELL

THE BLACK SNAKE

Black snake! Black snake!
Curling on the ground,
Rolled like a rubber tire,
Ribbed and round.
Black snake! Black snake!
Looped in a tree,
Limp as a licorice whip
Flung free.
Black snake! Black snake!
Curving down the lawn,
Glides like a wave
With its silver gone.
Black snake! Black snake!
Come and live with me!
I'll feed you and I'll pet you
And then I'll set you free!

PATRICIA HUBBELL

INDIA

They hunt, the velvet tigers in the jungle,
The spotted jungle full of shapeless patches—
Sometimes they're leaves, sometimes they're hanging flowers,
Sometimes they're hot gold patches of the sun:
They hunt, the velvet tigers in the jungle!

What do they hunt by glimmering pools of water,
By the round silver Moon, the Pool of Heaven—
In the striped grass, amid the barkless trees—
The stars scattered like eyes of beasts above them!

What do they hunt, their hot breath scorching insects,
Insects that blunder blindly in the way,
Vividly fluttering—they also are hunting,
Are glittering with a tiny ecstasy!

The grass is flaming and the trees are growing,
The very mud is gurgling in the pools,
Green toads are watching, crimson parrots flying,
Two pairs of eyes meet one another glowing—
They hunt, the velvet tigers in the jungle.

W. J. TURNER

BUFFALO DUSK

The buffaloes are gone.
And those who saw the buffaloes are gone.
Those who saw the buffaloes by thousands and how they
    pawed the prairie sod into dust with their great hoofs,
    their great heads down pawing on in a great pageant
    of dusk,
Those who saw the buffaloes are gone.
And the buffaloes are gone.

CARL SANDBURG

THE INTRUDER

Two-boots in the forest walks,
Pushing through the bracken stalks.

Vanishing like a puff of smoke,
Nimbletail flies up the oak.

Longears helter-skelter shoots
Into his house among the roots.

At work upon the highest bark,
Tapperbill knocks off to hark.

Painted-wings through sun and shade
Flounces off along the glade.

Not a creature lingers by,
When clumping Two-boots comes to pry.

JAMES REEVES

The wolf also shall dwell with the lamb,
And the leopard shall lie down with the kid;
And the calf and the young lion and the fatling together;
And a little child shall lead them.
And the cow and the bear shall feed;
Their young ones shall lie down together;
And the lion shall eat straw like the ox.
And the sucking child shall play on the hole of the asp,
And the weaned child shall put his hand on the cockatrice's den.
They shall not hurt nor destroy
In all my holy mountain:
For the earth shall be full of the knowledge of the Lord,
As the waters cover the sea.

THE BIBLE

Hurt no living thing:
Ladybird nor butterfly,
Nor moth with dusty wing,
Nor cricket chirping cheerily,
Nor grasshopper so light of leap,
Nor dancing gnat, nor beetle fat,
Nor harmless worms that creep.

CHRISTINA ROSSETTI

I think I could turn and live with animals, they are so placid
and self-contain'd,
I stand and look at them and long and long.
They do not sweat and whine about their condition,
They do not lie awake in the dark and weep for their sins,
They do not make me sick discussing their duty to God,
Not one is dissatisfied, not one is demented with the mania of
owning things,
Not one kneels to another, nor to his kind that lived thousands
of years ago,
Not one is respectable or unhappy over the whole earth.

WALT WHITMAN

LITTLE THINGS

Little things that run and quail
And die in silence and despair;

Little things that fight and fail
And fall on earth and sea and air;

All trapped and frightened little things,
The mouse, the coney, hear our prayer

As we forgive those done to us,
The lamb, the linnet, and the hare,

Forgive us all our trespasses,
Little creatures everywhere.

JAMES STEPHENS

11. "I know a place
that's oh, so green . . ."

A BOY'S PLACE

I know a place
that's oh, so green
where elephant ears
together lean;
a quiet place
that no one's seen
but me.

It's not very far
my secret spot.
I go whenever
the day's too hot
for friends or games
or a story's plot—
just me.

I leave my shoes
at home and go
over the wall
where the blackberries grow
and squoosh my toes
in the mud, with no
design.

A gentle jungle
of swamp and sky,
a curious bird

my only spy,
a place to whistle
each August by—
all mine!

ROSE BURGUNDER

GROWING UP

When I was seven
We went for a picnic
Up to a magic
Foresty place.
I knew there were tigers
Behind every boulder,
Though I didn't meet one
Face to face.

When I was older
We went for a picnic
Up to the very same
Place as before,
And all of the trees
And the rocks were so little
They couldn't hide tigers
Or *me* any more.

HARRY BEHN

THE WOOD OF FLOWERS

I went to the Wood of Flowers,
No one went with me;
I was there alone for hours;
I was happy as could be,
In the Wood of Flowers!

There was grass
On the ground;
There were leaves
On the tree;

And the wind
Had a sound
Of such sheer
Gaiety

That I
Was as happy
As happy could be,
In the Wood of Flowers!

JAMES STEPHENS

TIGER LILY

The tiger lily is a panther,
Orange to black spot:
Her tongue is the velvet pretty anther,
And she's in the vacant lot.

The cool day lilies grow beside her,
But they are done now and dead,
And between them a little silver spider
Hangs from a thread.

DAVID MC CORD

White coral bells upon a slender stalk,
Lilies of the valley deck my garden walk.

Oh, don't you wish that you could hear them ring?
That will happen only when the fairies sing.

AUTHOR UNKNOWN

DANDELION

O little soldier with the golden helmet,
What are you guarding on my lawn?
You with your green gun
And your yellow beard,
Why do you stand so stiff?
There is only the grass to fight!

HILDA CONKLING

FORMER BARN LOT

Once there was a fence here,
   And the grass came and tried—
Leaning from the pasture—
   To get inside.

But colt feet trampled it,
   Turning it brown,
Until the farmer moved
   And the fence fell down;

Then any bird saw,
   Under the wire,
Grass nibbling inward
   Like green fire.

MARK VAN DOREN

THE PASTURE

I'm going out to clean the pasture spring;
I'll only stop to rake the leaves away
(And wait to watch the water clear, I may);
I shan't be gone long.—You come too.

I'm going out to fetch the little calf
That's standing by the mother. It's so young
It totters when she licks it with her tongue.
I shan't be gone long.—You come too.

ROBERT FROST

STOPPING BY WOODS
ON A SNOWY EVENING

Whose woods these are I think I know.
His house is in the village though;
He will not see me stopping here
To watch his woods fill up with snow.

My little horse must think it queer
To stop without a farmhouse near
Between the woods and frozen lake
The darkest evening of the year.

He gives his harness bells a shake
To ask if there is some mistake.
The only other sound's the sweep
Of easy wind and downy flake.

The woods are lovely, dark and deep,
But I have promises to keep,
And miles to go before I sleep.
And miles to go before I sleep.

ROBERT FROST

ROADS

A road might lead to anywhere—
  To harbor towns and quays,
Or to a witch's pointed house
  Hidden by bristly trees.
It might lead past the tailor's door,
  Where he sews with needle and thread,
Or by Miss Pim the milliner's,
  With hats for every head.
It might be a road to a great, dark cave
  With treasure and gold piled high,
Or a road with a mountain tied to its end,
  Blue-humped against the sky.
Oh, a road might lead you anywhere—
  To Mexico or Maine.
But then, it might just fool you, and—
  Lead you back home again!

RACHEL FIELD

THIS IS MY ROCK

This is my rock,
And here I run
To steal the secret of the sun;

This is my rock,
And here come I
Before the night has swept the sky;

This is my rock,
This is the place
I meet the evening face to face.

DAVID MC CORD

Rushes in a watery place,
    And reeds in a hollow;
A soaring skylark in the sky,
    A darting swallow;
And where pale blossoms used to hang
    Ripe fruit to follow.

CHRISTINA ROSSETTI

AFTERNOON ON A HILL

I will be the gladdest thing
    Under the sun!
I will touch a hundred flowers
    And not pick one.

I will look at cliffs and clouds
    With quiet eyes,
Watch the wind blow down the grass,
    And the grass rise.

And when lights begin to show
    Up from the town,
I will mark which must be mine,
    And then start down!

EDNA ST. VINCENT MILLAY

All I could see from where I stood
Was three long mountains and a wood;
I turned and looked another way,
And saw three islands in a bay.
So with my eyes I traced the line
Of the horizon, thin and fine,
Straight around till I was come
Back to where I'd started from;
And all I saw from where I stood
Was three long mountains and a wood.
Over these things I could not see;
These were the things that bounded me;
And I could touch them with my hand,
Almost, I thought, from where I stand.

EDNA ST. VINCENT MILLAY

little tree
little silent Christmas tree
you are so little
you are more like a flower

who found you in the green forest
and were you sorry to come away?
see   i will comfort you
because you smell so sweetly

i will kiss your cool bark
and hug you safe and tight
just as your mother would,
only don't be afraid

look   the spangles
that sleep all the year in a dark box
dreaming of being taken out and allowed to shine,
the balls the chains red and gold the fluffy threads,

put up your little arms
and i'll give them all to you to hold
every finger shall have its ring
and there won't be a single place dark or unhappy

then when you're quite dressed
you'll stand in the window for everyone to see
and how they'll stare!
oh but you'll be very proud

and my little sister and i will take hands
and looking up at our beautiful tree
we'll dance and sing
"Noel Noel"

E. E. CUMMINGS

CHRISTMAS TREE

I'll find me a spruce
in the cold white wood
with wide green boughs
and a snowy hood.

I'll pin on a star
with five gold spurs
to mark my spruce
from the pines and firs.

I'll make me a score
of suet balls
to tie to my spruce
when the cold dusk falls,

And I'll hear next day
from the sheltering trees,
the Christmas carols
of the chickadees.

AILEEN FISHER

I believe a leaf of grass is no less than the journey-work of the
    stars,
And the pismire is equally perfect, and a grain of sand, and
    the egg of a wren,
And the tree-toad is the chef-d'oeuvre for the highest,
And the running blackberry would adorn the parlors of heaven,
And the narrowest hinge in my hand puts to scorn all machinery,
And the cow crunching with depress'd head surpasses any
    statue,
And a mouse is miracle enough to stagger sextillions of infidels.

WALT WHITMAN

12. "Yet there isn't a train I wouldn't take . . ."

TRAVEL

The railroad track is miles away,
　　And the day is loud with voices speaking,
Yet there isn't a train goes by all day
　　But I hear its whistles shrieking.

All night there isn't a train goes by,
　　Though the night is still for sleep and dreaming
But I see its cinders red on the sky
　　And hear its engine steaming.

My heart is warm with the friends I make,
　　And better friends I'll not be knowing,
Yet there isn't a train I wouldn't take,
　　No matter where it's going.

EDNA ST. VINCENT MILLAY

I like to see it lap the miles,
And lick the valleys up,
And stop to feed itself at tanks;
And then, prodigious, step

Around a pile of mountains,
And, supercilious, peer
In shanties by the sides of roads;
And then a quarry pare

To fit its sides, and crawl between,
Complaining all the while
In horrid, hooting stanza;
Then chase itself down hill

And neigh like Boanerges;
Then, punctual as a star,
Stop—docile and omnipotent—
At its own stable door.

EMILY DICKINSON

NIGHT TRAIN

A train at night
is yellow lights running
across the darkness
with a sound of many
black doors slamming
in a long hall,
one after another,
but softer,
and softer,
until the last one
whispers
and closes.

ADRIEN STOUTENBURG

A MODERN DRAGON

A train is a dragon that roars through the dark.
He wriggles his tail as he sends up a spark.
He pierces the night with his one yellow eye,
And all the earth trembles when he rushes by.

ROWENA BASTIN BENNETT

THE FREIGHT TRAIN

The slow freight wriggles along the rail
With a red caboose for a lashing tail,
With a one-eyed engine for a head
The slow freight follows the river bed.

He moves like a snake that has grown too fat,
One that has swallowed a frog and a rat;
But a giant of snakes is the moving freight
And these are some of the things he ate:

A herd of sheep and a hundred hens
And dozens of pigs with crates for pens
And horses and cows by the sixes and tens;
And these are some of the things he drank:
Oil and gasoline by the tank,
Milk by the gallon and cream by the pail—
No wonder he moves at the pace of a snail.

ROWENA BASTIN BENNETT

FROM A RAILWAY CARRIAGE

Faster than fairies, faster than witches,
Bridges and houses, hedges and ditches;
And charging along like troops in a battle,
All through the meadows the horses and cattle:
All of the sights of the hill and the plain
Fly as thick as driving rain;
And ever again, in the wink of an eye,
Painted stations whistle by.

Here is a child who clambers and scrambles,
All by himself and gathering brambles;
Here is a tramp who stands and gazes;
And there is the green for stringing the daisies!
Here is a cart run away in the road
Lumping along with man and load;
And here is a mill, and there is a river:
Each a glimpse and gone for ever!

ROBERT LOUIS STEVENSON

13. "I must go down to the seas again . . ."

I'D LIKE TO BE A LIGHTHOUSE

I'd like to be a lighthouse
    And scrubbed and painted white.
I'd like to be a lighthouse
    And stay awake all night
To keep my eye on everything
    That sails my patch of sea;
I'd like to be a lighthouse
    With the ships all watching me.

RACHEL FIELD

WARNING

The inside of a whirlpool
Is not a place to stop,
Or you'll find you reach the bottom
Before you reach the top.

JOHN CIARDI

THE RIVER IS A PIECE OF SKY

From the top of a bridge
The river below
Is a piece of sky—
      Until you throw
      A penny in
      Or a cockleshell
      Or a pebble or two
      Or a bicycle bell
      Or a cobblestone
      Or a fat man's cane—
And then you can see
It's a river again.

The difference you'll see
When you drop your penny:
The river has splashes,
The sky hasn't any.

JOHN CIARDI

WATER

The world turns softly
Not to spill its lakes and rivers.
The water is held in its arms
And the sky is held in the water.
What is water,
That pours silver,
And can hold the sky?

HILDA CONKLING

LOST

Desolate and lone
All night on the lake
Where fog trails and mist creeps,
The whistle of a boat
Calls and cries unendingly,
Like some lost child
In tears and trouble
Hunting the harbor's breast
And the harbor's eyes.

CARL SANDBURG

I must go down to the seas again, to the lonely sea and the sky,
And all I ask is a tall ship and a star to steer her by;
And the wheel's kick and the wind's song and the white sail's
    shaking,
And the gray mist on the sea's face, and a gray dawn breaking.

I must go down to the seas again, for the call of the running
    tide
Is a wild call and a clear call that may not be denied;
And all I ask is a windy day with the white clouds flying,
And the flung spray and the blown spume, and the seagulls
    crying.

I must go down to the seas again, to the vagrant gypsy life,
To the gull's way and the whale's way where the wind's like
    a whetted knife;
And all I ask is a merry yarn from a laughing fellow-rover,
And quiet sleep and a sweet dream when the long trick's over.

JOHN MASEFIELD

THE SEA GYPSY

I am fevered with the sunset,
I am fretful with the bay,
For the wander-thirst is on me
And my soul is in Cathay.

There's a schooner in the offing,
With her topsails shot with fire,
And my heart has gone aboard her
For the Islands of Desire.

I must forth again to-morrow!
With the sunset I must be
Hull down on the trail of rapture
In the wonder of the sea.

RICHARD HOVEY

14. "The city spreads its wings..."

CITY

In the morning the city
Spreads its wings
Making a song
In stone that sings.

In the evening the city
Goes to bed
Hanging lights
About its head.

LANGSTON HUGHES

CITY LIGHTS

Into the endless dark
The lights of the buildings shine,
Row upon twinkling row,
Line upon glistening line.
Up and up they mount
Till the tallest seems to be
The topmost taper set
On a towering Christmas tree.

RACHEL FIELD

WHEN YOU WALK

When you walk in a field,
Look down
Lest you trample
A daisy's crown!

But in a city
Look always high,
And watch
The beautiful clouds go by!

JAMES STEPHENS

MRS. PECK-PIGEON

Mrs. Peck-Pigeon
Is picking for bread,
Bob—bob—bob
Goes her little round head.
Tame as a pussy-cat
In the street,
Step—step—step
Go her little red feet.
With her little red feet
And her little round head,
Mrs. Peck-Pigeon
Goes picking for bread.

ELEANOR FARJEON

CITY TRAFFIC

Green as a seedling the one lane shines,
Red ripened blooms for the opposite lines;
Emerald shoot,
Vermilion fruit.

Now amber, now champagne, now honey: go slow:
Shift, settle, then gather and sow.

EVE MERRIAM

PEOPLE WHO MUST

I painted on the roof of a skyscraper.
I painted a long while and called it a day's work.
The people on a corner swarmed and the traffic cop's whistle
    never let up all afternoon.
They were the same as bugs, many bugs on their way—
Those people on the go or at a standstill;
And the traffic cop a spot of blue, a splinter of brass,
Where the black tides ran around him
And he kept the street. I painted a long while
And called it a day's work.

CARL SANDBURG

SMOKE ANIMALS

Out of the factory chimney, tall
Great black animals like to crawl.
They push each other and shove and crowd.
They nose the wind and they claw a cloud,
And they walk right out on the empty sky
With their tails all curled and their heads held high;
But their terrible fierceness is just a joke
For they're only made of a puff of smoke.

ROWENA BASTIN BENNETT

A TIME FOR BUILDING

A dozen machines
come roaring down,
tractors and shovels,
hydraulics and dumps,
mixers and graders,
diggers and pumps,

pushing and groaning and moving the road
to another place in town.

MYRA COHN LIVINGSTON

CONCRETE MIXERS

The drivers are washing the concrete mixers;
Like elephant tenders they hose them down.
Tough grey-skinned monsters standing ponderous,
Elephant-bellied and elephant-nosed,
Standing in muck up to their wheel-caps,
Like rows of elephants, tail to trunk.
Their drivers perch on their backs like mahouts,
Sending the sprays of water up.
They rid the trunk-like trough of concrete,
Direct the spray to the bulging sides,
Turn and start the monsters moving.
        Concrete mixers
        Move like elephants
        Bellow like elephants
        Spray like elephants,
    Concrete mixers are urban elephants,
    Their trunks are raising a city.

PATRICIA HUBBELL

BAM, BAM, BAM

Pickaxes, pickaxes swinging today,
Plaster clouds flying every which way.

Workmen are covered with white dust like snow,
Oh, come see the great demolition show!

Slam, slam, slam,
Goes the steel wrecking-ball;
Bam, bam, bam
Against a stone wall.

It's raining bricks and wood
In my neighborhood.
Down go the houses,
Down go the stores,
Up goes a building
With forty-seven floors.

Crash goes a chimney,
Pow goes a hall,
Zowie goes a doorway,
Zam goes a wall.

Slam, slam, slam,
Goes the steel wrecking-ball;
Bam, bam, bam,
Changing it all.

EVE MERRIAM

PRAYERS OF STEEL

Lay me on an anvil, O God.
Beat me and hammer me into a crowbar.
Let me pry loose old walls;
Let me lift and loosen old foundations.

Lay me on an anvil, O God.
Beat me and hammer me into a steel spike.
Drive me into the girders that hold a skyscraper together.
Take red-hot rivets and fasten me into the central girders.
Let me be the great nail holding a skyscraper through blue
    nights into white stars.

CARL SANDBURG

15. "I was one of the children told . . ."

A PECK OF GOLD

Dust always blowing about the town,
Except when sea-fog laid it down,
And I was one of the children told
Some of the blowing dust was gold.

All the dust the wind blew high
Appeared like gold in the sunset sky,
But I was one of the children told
Some of the dust was really gold.

Such was life in the Golden Gate:
Gold dusted all we drank and ate,
And I was one of the children told,
"We all must eat our peck of gold."

ROBERT FROST

"Ferry me across the water,
　Do, boatman, do."
"If you've a penny in your purse
　I'll ferry you."

"I have a penny in my purse,
　And my eyes are blue;
So ferry me across the water,
　Do, boatman, do."

"Step into my ferry-boat,
　Be they black or blue,
And for the penny in your purse
　I'll ferry you."

CHRISTINA ROSSETTI

SWEEPING THE SKY

There was an old woman tossed up in a basket,
Ninety times as high as the moon;
And where was she going, I couldn't but ask it
For in her hand she carried a broom.

"Old woman, old woman, old woman." quoth I,
"Whither, O whither, O whither so high?"
"To sweep the cobwebs off the sky!"
"Shall I go with you?" "Aye, by-and-by."

AUTHOR UNKNOWN

FIVE LITTLE CHICKENS

Said the first little chicken,
  With a queer little squirm,
"I wish I could find
  A fat little worm."

Said the next little chicken,
  With an odd little shrug,
"I wish I could find
  A fat little slug."

Said the third little chicken,
  With a sharp little squeal,
"I wish I could find
  Some nice yellow meal."

Said the fourth little chicken,
  With a small sigh of grief,
"I wish I could find
  A little green leaf."

Said the fifth little chicken,
  With a faint little moan,
"I wish I could find
  A wee gravel stone."

"Now, see here," said the mother,
  From the green garden patch,
"If you want any breakfast,
  Just come here and scratch."

AUTHOR UNKNOWN

THE LIGHT-HOUSE-KEEPER'S
WHITE-MOUSE

As I rowed out to the light-house
For a cup of tea one day,
I came on a very wet white-mouse
Out swimming in the bay.

"If you are for the light-house,"
Said he, "I'm glad we met.
I'm the light-house-keeper's white-mouse
And I fear I'm getting wet."

"O light-house-keeper's white-mouse,
I am rowing out for tea
With the keeper in his light-house.
Let me pull you in with me."

So I gave an oar to the white-mouse.
And I pulled on the other.
And we all had tea at the light-house
With the keeper and his mother.

JOHN CIARDI

They fished and they fished
Way down in the sea,
Down in the sea a mile,
They fished among all the fish in the sea
For the fish with the deep sea smile.

One fish came up from the deep of the sea,
From down in the sea a mile,
It had blue green eyes
And whiskers three
But never a deep sea smile.

One fish came up from the deep of the sea,
From down in the sea a mile,
With electric lights up and down his tail
But never a deep sea smile.

They fished and they fished
Way down in the sea,
Down in the sea a mile,
They fished among all the fish in the sea
For the fish with the deep sea smile.

One fish came up with terrible teeth,
One fish with long strong jaws,
One fish came up with long stalked eyes,
One fish with terrible claws.

They fished all through the ocean deep
For many and many a mile,
And they caught a fish with a laughing eye
But none with a deep sea smile.

And then one day they got a pull
From down in the sea a mile,
And when they pulled the fish into the boat
He smiled a deep sea smile.

And as he smiled, the hook got free
And then, what a deep sea smile!
He flipped his tail and swam away
Down in the sea a mile.

MARGARET WISE BROWN

THE FLATTERED FLYING FISH

Said the Shark to the Flying Fish over the phone:
"Will you join me tonight? I am dining alone.
Let me order a nice little dinner for two!
And come as you are in your shimmering blue!"

Said the Flying Fish: "Fancy remembering me,
And the dress that I wore at the Porpoises' tea!"
"How could I forget?" said the Shark in his guile:
"I expect you at eight!" and rang off with a smile.

She has powdered her nose; she has put on her things;
She is off with one flap of her luminous wings.
O little one, lovely, light-hearted and vain,
The Moon will not shine on your beauty again!

E. V. RIEU

THE SHIP OF RIO

There was a ship of Rio
   Sailed out into the blue,
And nine and ninety monkeys
   Were all her jovial crew.
From bo'sun to the cabin boy,
   From quarter to caboose,
There weren't a stitch of calico
   To breech 'em—tight or loose;
From spar to deck, from deck to keel,
   From barnacle to shroud,
There weren't one pair of reach-me-downs
   To all that jabbering crowd.
But wasn't it a gladsome sight,
   When roared the deep-sea gales,
To see them reef her fore and aft,
   A-swinging by their tails!
Oh, wasn't it a gladsome sight,
   When glassy calm did come,
To see them squatting tailor-wise
   Around a keg of rum!
Oh, wasn't it a gladsome sight,
   When in she sailed to land,
To see them all a-scampering skip
   For nuts across the sand!

WALTER DE LA MARE

THE OWL AND THE PUSSY-CAT

I

The Owl and the Pussy-Cat went to sea
    In a beautiful pea-green boat,
They took some honey, and plenty of money,
    Wrapped up in a five-pound note.
The Owl looked up to the stars above,
    And sang to a small guitar,
"O lovely Pussy! O Pussy, my love,
    What a beautiful Pussy you are,
        You are,
        You are!
    What a beautiful Pussy you are!"

II

Pussy said to the Owl, "You elegant fowl!
    How charmingly sweet you sing!
O let us be married! too long we have tarried:
    But what shall we do for a ring?"
They sailed away for a year and a day,
    To the land where the Bong-tree grows,
And there in a wood a Piggy-wig stood,
    With a ring at the end of his nose,
        His nose,
        His nose,
    With a ring at the end of his nose.

III

"Dear Pig, are you willing to sell for one shilling
   Your ring?" Said the Piggy, "I will."
So they took it away, and were married next day
   By the Turkey who lives on the hill.
They dined on mince, and slices of quince,
   Which they ate with a runcible spoon;
And hand in hand, on the edge of the sand,
   They danced by the light of the moon,
     The moon,
     The moon,
   They danced by the light of the moon.

EDWARD LEAR

BUCKINGHAM PALACE

They're changing guard at Buckingham Palace—
Christopher Robin went down with Alice.
Alice is marrying one of the guard.
"A soldier's life is terrible hard,"
                                                Says Alice.

They're changing guard at Buckingham Palace—
Christopher Robin went down with Alice.
We saw a guard in a sentry-box.
"One of the sergeants looks after their socks,"
                                                Says Alice.

They're changing guard at Buckingham Palace—
Christopher Robin went down with Alice.
We looked for the King, but he never came.
"Well, God take care of him, all the same,"
                                                Says Alice.

They're changing guard at Buckingham Palace—
Christopher Robin went down with Alice.
They've great big parties inside the grounds.
"I wouldn't be King for a hundred pounds,"
                                        Says Alice.

They're changing guard at Buckingham Palace—
Christopher Robin went down with Alice.
A face looked out, but it wasn't the King's.
"He's much too busy a-signing things,"
                                        Says Alice.

They're changing guard at Buckingham Palace—
Christopher Robin went down with Alice.
"Do you think the King knows all about *me*?"
"Sure to, dear, but it's time for tea,"
                                        Says Alice.

                                A. A. MILNE

THE BLACK PEBBLE

There went three children down to the shore,
    Down to the shore and back;
There was skipping Susan and bright-eyed Sam
    And little scowling Jack.

Susan found a white cockle-shell,
    The prettiest ever seen,
And Sam picked up a piece of glass
    Rounded and smooth and green.

But Jack found only a plain black pebble
    That lay by the rolling sea,
And that was all that ever he found;
    So back they went all three.

The cockle-shell they put on the table,
    The green glass on the shelf,
But the little black pebble that Jack had found,
    He kept it for himself.

JAMES REEVES

THE ONE ANSWER

On yonder hill there stands a creature,
  Who she is I do not know.
I'll go ask her hand in marriage,
  And she'll answer yes or no.
"O, no, John; no, John; no, John, no!"

"My father was a Spanish captain,
  Went to sea a year ago;
First he kissed me, then he left me,
  Bade me always answer no.
So no, John; no, John; no, John, no."

Madam, in your face is beauty;
  On your lips red roses grow.
Will you take me for your husband?
  Madam, answer yes or no.
"O, no, John; no, John; no, John, no."

Madam, since you are so cruel,
  And since you do scorn me so,
If I may not be your husband,
  Madam, will you let me go?
"O, no, John; no, John; no, John, no."

Hark! I hear the church-bells ringing;
  Will you come and be my wife?
Or, dear madam, have you settled
  To live single all your life?
"O, no, John; no, John; no, John, no!"

AUTHOR UNKNOWN

THE OLD WIFE AND THE GHOST

There was an old wife and she lived all alone
   In a cottage not far from Hitchin:
And one bright night, by the full moon light,
   Comes a ghost right into her kitchen.

About that kitchen neat and clean
   The ghost goes pottering round.
But the poor old wife is deaf as a boot
   And so hears never a sound.

The ghost blows up the kitchen fire,
   As bold as bold can be;
He helps himself from the larder shelf,
   But never a sound hears she.

He blows on his hands to make them warm,
   And whistles aloud "Whee-hee!"
But still as a sack the old soul lies
   And never a sound hears she.

From corner to corner he runs about,
   And into the cupboard he peeps;
He rattles the door and bumps on the floor,
   But still the old wife sleeps.

Jangle and bang go the pots and pans,
   As he throws them all around;
And the plates and mugs and dishes and jugs,
   He flings them all to the ground.

Madly the ghost tears up and down
   And screams like a storm at sea;
And at last the old wife stirs in her bed—
   And it's "Drat those mice," says she.

Then the first cock crows and morning shows
   And the troublesome ghost's away.
But oh! what a pickle the poor wife sees
   When she gets up next day.

"Them's tidy big mice," the old wife thinks,
   And off she goes to Hitchin,
And a tidy big cat she fetches back
   To keep the mice from her kitchen.

JAMES REEVES

LITTLE JOHN BOTTLEJOHN

Little John Bottlejohn lived on the hill,
   And a blithe little man was he.
And he won the heart of a pretty mermaid
   Who lived in the deep blue sea.
And every evening she used to sit
   And sing by the rocks of the sea,
"Oh! little John Bottlejohn, pretty John Bottlejohn,
   Won't you come out to me?"

Little John Bottlejohn heard her song,
   And he opened his little door,
And he hopped and he skipped, and he skipped and he hopped,
   Until he came down to the shore.
And there on the rocks sat the little mermaid,
   And still she was singing so free,
"Oh! little John Bottlejohn, pretty John Bottlejohn,
   Won't you come out to me?"

Little John Bottlejohn made a bow,
  And the mermaid, she made one too;
And she said, "Oh! I never saw anyone half
  So perfectly sweet as you!
In my lovely home 'neath the ocean foam,
  How happy we both might be!
Oh! little John Bottlejohn, pretty John Bottlejohn,
  Won't you come down with me?"

Little John Bottlejohn said, "Oh yes!
  I'll willingly go with you,
And I never shall quail at the sight of your tail,
  For perhaps I may grow one, too."
So he took her hand, and he left the land,
  And plunged in the foaming main.
And little John Bottlejohn, pretty John Bottlejohn,
  Never was seen again.

LAURA E. RICHARDS

It fell about the Martinmas time,
   And a gay time it was then,
When our goodwife got puddings to make,
   And she's boiled them in the pan.

The wind so cold blew south and north,
   And blew into the floor;
Quoth our goodman to our goodwife,
   "Get up and bar the door."

"My hand is in my household work,
   Goodman, as ye may see;
And it will not be barred for a hundred years,
   If it's to be barred by me!"

They made a pact between them both,
   They made it firm and sure,
That whosoe'er should speak the first,
   Should rise and bar the door.

Then by there came two gentlemen,
   At twelve o'clock at night,
And they could see neither house nor hall,
   Nor coal nor candlelight.

"Now whether is this a rich man's house
   Or whether is it a poor?"
But never a word would one of them speak,
   For barring of the door.

The guests they ate the white puddings,
    And then they ate the black;
Tho' much the goodwife thought to herself,
    Yet never a word she spake.

Then said one stranger to the other,
    "Here, man, take ye my knife;
Do ye take off the old man's beard,
    And I'll kiss the goodwife."

"There's no hot water to scrape it off,
    And what shall we do then?"
"Then why not use the pudding broth,
    That boils into the pan?"

O up then started our goodman,
    An angry man was he;
"Will ye kiss my wife before my eyes!
    And with pudding broth scald me!"

Then up and started our goodwife,
    Gave three skips on the floor;
"Goodman, you've spoken the very first word!
    Get up and bar the door!"

AUTHOR UNKNOWN

The King walked in his garden green,
　Where grew a marvellous tree;
And out of its leaves came singing birds
　By one, and two, and three.

The first bird had wings of white,
　The second had wings of gold,
The third had wings of deepest blue
　Most beauteous to behold.

The white bird flew to the northern land,
　The gold bird flew to the west,
The blue bird flew to the cold, cold south
　Where never bird might nest.

The King waited a twelvemonth long,
　Till back the three birds flew,
They lighted down upon the tree,
　The white, the gold, and the blue.

The white bird brought a pearly seed
　And gave it to the King;
The gold bird from out of the west
　He brought a golden ring.

The third bird with feathers blue
　Who came from the far cold south,
A twisted sea-shell smooth and grey
　He carried in his mouth.

The King planted the pearly seed
   Down in his garden green,
And up there sprang a pearl-white maid,
   The fairest ever seen.

She looked at the King and knelt her down
   All under the magic tree,
She smiled at him with her red lips
   But not a word said she.

Instead she took the grey sea-shell
   And held it to his ear,
She pressed it close and soon the King
   A strange, sweet song did hear.

He raised the fair maid by the hand
   Until she stood at his side;
Then he gave her the golden ring
   And took her for his bride.

And at their window sang the birds,
   They sang the whole night through,
Then off they went at break of day,
   The white, the gold, and the blue.

JAMES REEVES

JOHNNIE CRACK AND FLOSSIE SNAIL

Johnnie Crack and Flossie Snail
Kept their baby in a milking pail
Flossie Snail and Johnnie Crack
One would pull it out and one would put it back.

O it's my turn now said Flossie Snail
To take the baby from the milking pail
And it's my turn now said Johnnie Crack
To smack it on the head and put it back.

Johnnie Crack and Flossie Snail
Kept their baby in a milking pail
One would put it back and one would pull it out
And all it had to drink was ale and stout
For Johnnie Crack and Flossie Snail
Always used to say that stout and ale
Was *good* for a baby in a milking pail.

                              DYLAN THOMAS

16. "A dozen dreams to dance to you . . ."

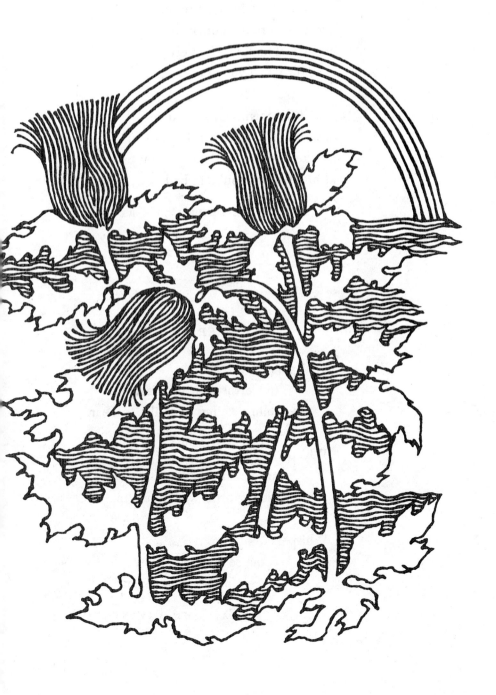

KEEP A POEM IN YOUR POCKET

Keep a poem in your pocket
and a picture in your head
and you'll never feel lonely
at night when you're in bed.

The little poem will sing to you
and the little picture bring to you
a dozen dreams to dance to you
at night when you're in bed.

BEATRICE SCHENK DE REGNIERS

WHISPERS

Whispers
    tickle through your ear
    telling things you like to hear.

Whispers
    are as soft as skin
    letting little words curl in.

Whispers
    come so they can blow
    secrets others never know.

MYRA COHN LIVINGSTON

A PIPER

A piper in the streets to-day
Set up, and tuned, and started to play,
And away, away, away on the tide
Of his music we started; on every side
Doors and windows were opened wide,
And men left down their work and came,
And women with petticoats coloured like flame.
And little bare feet that were blue with cold,
Went dancing back to the age of gold,
And all the world went gay, went gay,
For half an hour in the street to-day.

SEUMAS O'SULLIVAN

I'm nobody! Who are you?
Are you nobody too?
Then there's a pair of us—don't tell!
They'd banish us, you know.

How dreary to be somebody!
How public, like a frog
To tell your name the livelong day
To an admiring bog.

EMILY DICKINSON

THE SECRET SONG

Who saw the petals
   drop from the rose?
I, said the spider,
But nobody knows.

Who saw the sunset
   flash on the bird?
I, said the fish,
But nobody heard.

Who saw the fog
   come over the sea?
I, said the pigeon,
Only me.

Who saw the first
   green light of the sun?
I, said the night owl,
The only one.

Who saw the moss
   creep over the stone?
I, said the grey fox,
All alone.

MARGARET WISE BROWN

THE SORCERESS!

I asked her, "Is Aladdin's lamp
Hidden anywhere?"
"Look into your heart," she said,
"Aladdin's lamp is there."

She took my heart with glowing hands.
It burned to dust and air
And smoke and rolling thistledown
Blowing everywhere.

"Follow the thistledown," she said,
"Till doomsday, if you dare,
Over the hills and far away.
Aladdin's lamp is there."

VACHEL LINDSAY

ONLY BE WILLING TO SEARCH FOR POETRY . . .

Only be willing to search for poetry, and there will be poetry:
My soul, a tiny speck, is my tutor.
Evening sun and fragrant grass are common things,
But, with understanding, they can become glorious verse.

YUAN MEI

Index of Authors and Titles

Index of Authors and Titles

Index of First Lines

Index of First Lines

Acknowledgments

Acknowledgments

"The Clown" and "On A Snowy Day" by Dorothy Aldis: Reprinted by permission of G. P. Putnam's Sons from *All Together* by Dorothy Aldis; Copyright 1925–1928, 1952 by Dorothy Aldis.

"The Fairies" by William Allingham: Reprinted with permission of The Macmillan Company from *Robin Redbreast and Other Poems* by William Allingham. Copyright 1930 by The Macmillan Company.

"The Hairy Dog" by Herbert Asquith: Reprinted with permission of The Macmillan Company from *Pillicock Hill* by Herbert Asquith. First published by The Macmillan Company in 1926. Reprinted by permission of William Heinemann Ltd.

"Grizzly Bear" by Mary Austin: Reprinted from *The Children Sing in the Far West* by Kenneth C. Chapman and Mary C. Wheelwright. Copyright © 1956 by Kenneth M. Chapman and Mary C. Wheelwright and reprinted by permission of the publishers, Houghton Mifflin Company.

"The Gnome" by Harry Behn: from *Windy Morning*, copyright, 1953, by Harry Behn. Reprinted by permission of Harcourt, Brace & World, Inc.

"Growing Up," "Hallowe'en" and "Mr. Pyme" by Harry Behn: From *The Little Hill*, copyright, 1949, by Harry Behn. Reprinted by permission of Harcourt, Brace & World, Inc.

"Over the wintry . . .": from *Cricket Songs: Japanese Haiku*, translated and © 1964 by Harry Behn. Reprinted by permission of Harcourt, Brace & World, Inc., and Curtis Brown Ltd.

"Some say the sun is a golden earring" and "The dark gray clouds" by Natalia M. Belting: From *The Sun Is a Golden Earring* by Natalia M. Belting. Copyright © 1962 by Natalia Belting. Reprinted by permission of Holt, Rinehart and Winston, Inc.

"The Freight Train" and "Smoke Animals" by Rowena Bennett: Reprinted by permission of the author.

"A Modern Dragon" by Rowena Bennett: From *Songs Around a Toadstool Table* by Rowena Bastin Bennett. Copyright © 1930, 1937, 1965 by Follett Publishing Co.

"Otto" and "Rudolph Is Tired of the City" by Gwendolyn Brooks: From *Bronzeville Boys and Girls* by Gwendolyn Brooks. Copyright © 1956 by Gwendolyn Brooks Blakely. Reprinted with permission of Harper & Row, Publishers.

"Pete at the Zoo" by Gwendolyn Brooks: From *The Bean Eaters* by Gwendolyn Brooks. Copyright © 1960 by Gwendolyn Brooks. Reprinted with permission of Harper & Row, Publishers.

"Jonathan Bing" by Beatrice Curtis Brown: Reprinted from *Jonathan Bing and Other Verses* by Beatrice Curtis Brown by permission of Lothrop, Lee & Shepard

the book *The Collected Poems of Theodore Roethke*. Reprinted by permission of Doubleday & Company, Inc.

"Who Has Seen the Wind" by Christina Rossetti: Reprinted with permission of The Macmillan Company from *Sing-Song* by Christina Rossetti. Copyright 1924 by The Macmillan Company.

"Auctioneer," "Bee Song" and "Daybreak" by Carl Sandburg: © 1960 by Carl Sandburg. Reprinted from his volume *Wind Song*, by permission of Harcourt, Brace & World, Inc.

"Buffalo Dusk" and "People Who Must" by Carl Sandburg: From *Smoke and Steel* by Carl Sandburg, copyright, 1920, by Harcourt, Brace & World, Inc. Reprinted by permission of the publishers.

"Lost" by Carl Sandburg: From *Chicago Poems* by Carl Sandburg. Copyright 1916 by Holt, Rinehart and Winston, Inc. Copyright 1944 by Carl Sandburg. Reprinted by permission of Holt, Rinehart and Winston, Inc. and Laurence Pollinger Limited.

"Prayers of Steel" by Carl Sandburg: From *Cornhuskers* by Carl Sandburg. Copyright 1918 by Holt, Rinehart and Winston, Inc. Copyright 1946 by Carl Sandburg. Reprinted by permission of Holt, Rinehart and Winston, Inc. and Laurence Pollinger Limited.

"Four Little Foxes" by Lew Saratt: From *Covenant with Earth* by Lew Saratt. Edited and copyrighted, 1956, by Alma Johnson Saratt. Gainesville: University of Florida Press, 1956.

"On Christmas Morn—Words from an Old Spanish Carol" by Ruth Sawyer: From *The Long Christmas* by Ruth Sawyer. Copyright 1941 by Ruth Sawyer. Reprinted by permission of The Viking Press, Inc.

"The Mouse in the Wainscot" by Ian Serraillier: From *The Tale of the Monster Horse* by Ian Serraillier. Reprinted by permission of Oxford University Press, London.

"Beware, My Child" by Shel Silverstein: Reprinted by permission of the author.

"Moon" and "The Owl" by William Jay Smith: Copyright, 1955, by William Jay Smith. From *Laughing in Time* by William Jay Smith, by permission of Atlantic-Little, Brown and Co. and Faber and Faber Ltd.

"Don't Ever Cross a Crocodile," "Eat-It-All Elaine," "Flying" and "Horse-Chestnut Time" by Kaye Starbird: From *Don't Ever Cross a Crocodile* by Kaye Starbird. Copyright © 1963 by Kaye Starbird. Published by J. B. Lippincott Company.

"Little Things" and "When You Walk" by James Stephens: Reprinted with permission of The Macmillan Company from *Collected Things* by James Stephens. Copyright 1926 by The Macmillan Company, renewed 1954 by Cynthia Stephens. Reprinted by permission of Mrs. Iris Wise, The Macmillan Company of Canada Limited and Macmillan & Co., Ltd.

"The Snare" and "The Wood of Flowers" by James Stephens: Reprinted with permission of The Macmillan Company from *Collected Poems* by James Stephens. Copyright 1915 by The Macmillan Company; renewed 1943 by James Stephens. Reprinted by permission of Mrs. Iris Wise, The Macmillan Company of Canada Limited and Macmillan & Co., Ltd.

"Night Train" and "Rain" by Adrien Stoutenburg: Reprinted from *The Things*

ABOUT THE AUTHOR

NANCY LARRICK is a distinguished educator, author, and editor. She has written numerous books and articles for parents and teachers, including the classic *A Parent's Guide to Children's Reading*. She has compiled fifteen anthologies of poetry for young readers, including *On City Streets, Room for Me and a Mountain Lion, I Heard a Scream in the Street,* and *When the Dark Comes Dancing*. Ms. Larrick lives in Winchester, Virginia.

ABOUT THE ILLUSTRATOR

ELLEN RASKIN was an artist of exceptional ability whose talent was heightened by a remarkably imaginative sense of humor. A prolific writer as well, her book *The Westing Game* won the Newbery Medal.